WHAT DO YOU MEAN

I CAN'T

PARK HERE?!

WHAT DO YOU MEAN

I CAN'T

PARK HERE?!

Love, Faith, Family, Freedom, and the Pursuit of Happiness

Don't let anyone tell you that you can't change the world

MICHAEL HERRMANN

DEFIANCE PRESS
& PUBLISHING

What Do You Mean I Can't Park Here?!

Printed in the United States of America

10 9 8 7 6 5 4 3 2 1

This book is a work of non-fiction. The author has made every effort to ensure that the accuracy of the information in this book was correct at the time of publication. Neither the author nor the publisher nor any other person(s) associated with this book may be held liable for any damages that may result from any of the ideas made by the author in this book.

DEFIANCE PRESS
& PUBLISHING

ISBN-13: 978-1-955937-24-5 (Paperback)
ISBN-13: 978-1-955937-25-2 (eBook)

Published by Defiance Press and Publishing, LLC

Bulk orders of this book may be obtained by contacting Defiance Press and Publishing, LLC at: www.defiancepress.com.

Public Relations Dept. – Defiance Press & Publishing, LLC
281-581-9300
pr@defiancepress.com

Defiance Press & Publishing, LLC
281-581-9300
info@defiancepress.com

THIS BOOK IS WRITTEN IN HONOR OF:
Arnold Riemer Sr.,
My Grandfather

DEDICATED TO:
My Wife and Children,
Jennifer, Brandon, Lucas, and Lauren

TABLE OF CONTENTS

INTRODUCTION

MOST OF US DON'T WILLINGLY go to the hospital. Generally, we go to the hospital if we are dealing with some sort of extremely painful or unpleasant experience in life. Thus, for most, a trip to the hospital is not considered a fun experience. Having a baby might be considered the one exception. For most families, this is a wonderful experience filled with excitement as the family comes together to celebrate new life and renewed hope for the future. Yet, all the while, the mother might be in great pain. The rush to the hospital with a woman in labor is often a very tangible reminder that a great many things can go wrong in this process. There is always a mix of excitement and fear until the baby is delivered and we hear the first cry.

Typically, a patient is dropped off at the hospital entrance, where staff will offer a wheelchair or other assistance. Hospitals build entrances specifically to insure there is plenty of space for several vehicles at a time to pull up, unload, and leave. That is, of course, the purpose: pull up, unload, and leave. A car parked at the entrance for any period of time prevents someone else from getting where they need to go.

You will often see uniformed security guards at hospitals patrolling the entrances to make sure people don't park at the entrance for any length of time. Some people will park at the entrance to go into the pharmacy rather than park in the parking lot. Some will park at the entry and wait for a patient for an hour rather than find a proper space in the parking lot. The standard approach for security officers confronting someone parked at a hospital entrance usually goes something like this:

Security - "Hi, how are you doing today?"

Driver - "Fine, why?"

Security - "Are you waiting for someone today?"

Driver - "Yes."

At this point, there is usually a moment of silence as the security officer waits for the driver to continue with some explanation of who he is waiting for. The officer assumes that the driver must understand he is asking this question for a reason. Meanwhile, the driver often seems to assume that whatever he is waiting for is none of the officer's business. The conversation continues:

Security - "Can I ask who you are waiting for?"

Driver - "My wife went into the pharmacy to pick up a prescription."

Security - "Oh, I hope she feels better soon."

Driver - "It's not for her, it's for me. She is fine."

Security - "Well, I hope you feel better soon, but you can't park here. You will need to pull out and go around the block. When you see her, you can pull back up to the entrance. Sorry."

Driver - "What do you mean I can't park here?!"

Security - "Sir, there is a five minute limit at the entrance. You have already been here for ten minutes, and there are a lot of other vehicles waiting for a chance to pull up and drop off a sick person. We need to keep traffic flowing."

Driver - "She will be out in a minute!"

Security - "Sir, that may be, but we need to be consistent with everyone. You will need to move along."

Driver -   "Don't you have something better to do than harass sick people?!"

This driver, who is unwilling to see the needs of others, will complain on his next trip to the hospital if he sees someone else sitting at the entrance. We would usually hear something like, "You were harassing me the last time I was here, and now I see someone else sitting out there. Why don't you do your job?!"

Oftentimes these people are in pain. They may be facing a life-altering healthcare crisis. Many are fearful of what the next few hours of life may bring. Under such circumstances, it is difficult to focus on anything else in life. People often become very angry, rude, belligerent, and hostile in these situations. This is understandable given the circumstances many may be facing, but it is still very frustrating being on the receiving end of such hostility. Healthcare professionals all over the world learn to be sensitive to people's pain and situations, but they must also develop a thick skin. If you want to work in healthcare for any period of time, you must possess an inherent compassion and love for others that can look past the hostility you often receive from the same people. This can be very difficult for even the most compassionate people to maintain when we consider the fact that many of these healthcare workers have our own stressful circumstances to deal with.

After years of working with people from all walks of life in some of the worst circumstances many of them will ever face, the desire to serve has developed into a sincere desire to understand why people behave the way they do. The core of a genuine customer service mentality is the desire to understand what others are thinking and feeling so we can say and do the right things to help them through difficult circumstances. Again, this requires compassion and patience, now more so than ever. Why, you ask? Because things are changing in our nation. There are a great many reasons to be frustrated in America. Yet more and more, we seem to forget that we have a lot to be grateful for.

I understand what to expect when working with people under stress. At the same time, I can't help but come to a very distinct conclusion: There are a lot of deeply unhappy people in America. Having said that, one can't help but ask, "Why?" Thus begins our discussion.

We spend our lives searching for an understanding of our life's purpose. For most, this seems to become a search for true love, the belief that the path to finding happiness in life involves finding that special someone who loves you through thick and thin, no matter what. Unfortunately, I don't think many of us find it—true love or purpose, that is.

Many of us have a desire to do more. Our day-to-day lives seem to consist of going to work, spending time with family, and having some fun with friends once in a while. The truth is that this amounts to a pretty good life. If you have a good job and a healthy, happy family, you have a lot to be thankful for. That's more than a lot of people have. If you have the means and opportunity to enjoy time with good friends, you can be very thankful for that as well. No one should feel guilt for having a lot to be thankful for. The problem is that most of us seem to have the lingering feeling that there is still more to life.

Everyone needs to work. If you want to have a roof over your head and food on your plate, you need to make money. If you really want to be truly successful in life, you need to find a career, not just a job. A career is a job you enjoy doing no matter which employer you work for. A career is work that gives you a sense of accomplishment beyond completion of the day's required assignments. When you enjoy going to work each day, you can take pride in what you do and know you are accomplishing something that makes a difference in people's lives.

Many Americans strive for this for years, believing they will someday find some peace or satisfaction in life once they have worked hard enough to become "successful." Most of the time, these same people do, in fact, reach the point of having what we would consider a "successful" career, but it still isn't enough to provide them with a sense of peace in life. The result? Their focus shifts from wanting to become successful to becoming wealthy.

When we can't find satisfaction in accomplishing something, we try to find comfort in the things we have—"When I can buy whatever I want, I will be happy" or "I will find some peace of mind when I don't have to worry about the bills anymore." Do these statements sound familiar? Have you thought this before? The old saying "Money does not buy happiness" is true; many of the wealthiest people in the world are still just as miserable as the rest of us.

Most of us can find an example of the truth in this statement within our own families. Even more so, we often see examples of this truth playing out on the five and ten o'clock news. Every evening we are given the latest details of the wealthy tycoons and entertainment moguls who were arrested, filed for divorce, or went into chemical dependency treatment.

For those of us in the low- to middle-class tax brackets living paycheck to paycheck, we look at these people and see wealth, glamour, and, according to our own beliefs about money, what *should* be happiness. However, when we look beyond their material possessions, we see that the people who should be happy seem to be just as lost as we are.

Even if you don't have a career yet, you still need a job. Work is an essential part of life. Even a criminal understands the fact that you don't make money unless you work for it. The harder you work, the more money you make, right? Well, not always. Oftentimes, the most successful among us have realized that it is more important to work better rather than just working harder. Work is essential, but how do you find satisfaction in life if you don't find it at work? Look for happiness after work, right? Some of us go home after work, and some of us go to the bar.

Without a doubt, it is fun to spend time with friends, dance, and have a couple of drinks. If this is your only glimpse of happiness in life, though, you will develop a constant need for this activity. Spending every evening at the bar or the club just leads to hangovers, addictions, and even greater loneliness. You will find yourself spending all of your hard-earned money on other people who disappear as soon as the money runs out or perhaps wake up naked in bed with a stranger with the sinking feeling of "Oh Lord, what did I do?" You never really experience happiness this way. Your problems never go away, and neither does the loneliness.

Entertainment does not fix the problems you face in life; it only allows you to avoid the problems for a few hours. After the booze and drugs wear off, reality hits. You will realize that the problems you sought to escape are still there. You'll feel guilt, and this makes everything worse than it was before. So, where do we find happiness and peace if we can't find this at work or at the bar? The answer is simple. We find peace, love, and happiness at home with our families. For many Americans, this is just a dream.

To live a healthy life, we need to find happiness and peace at home. Home is where we find the people who care about us. Home is not just a building; it is wherever we provide a safe place for our loved ones to lay their heads. If you don't feel comfortable going home, you will naturally feel lost. If we have problems at home, oftentimes we are the ones who created them, and our children are the ones who usually suffer the most for our mistakes.

Over the last several decades, the public school systems, along with a variety of special interest groups, have attempted a grand social experiment. They have attempted to replace the importance of family, of mom and dad, with the "It takes a village" principle of a community raising children. What they are really trying to say is that parents don't really know what is best for their children, but certain educated "experts" do. These experts don't pay for my child's food. They've never watched my child's face light up while opening a birthday present I picked out. They didn't wipe the dirt out of a skinned knee and a tear from a cheek after my child fell off the monkey bars. I did.

Children in modern America are raised in something of an assembly line, and this has done nothing more than give us higher rates of teen pregnancy, juvenile drug and alcohol use, juvenile crime, gang violence, and school shootings. The greatest atrocity in all of this is that the kids know exactly what is going on. Parents nowadays care more about their careers than they do about their children. As a result, the kids don't really care about themselves either.

The question we are left with is this: What do we do now? How do parents find a balance between work and family? How do we make the most of what little time we have to truly make sure our daughters and sons know we love them? It's important to recognize that you won't accomplish much by just spending less time at work. The fact of the matter is that most parents don't know how to be parents because they grew up in the same type of environment. Our children are looking for the same things we are: love, happiness, comfort, peace. We as adults have not found the love and peace we desire in life, and as such, we have no clue how to help our children find it either.

The simple truth is that you will never find love and peace in life by simply looking for love and peace. The only way to find what you are looking for is to search for an understanding of our higher purpose in life. You need to see the big picture by looking at your life as if looking down at it from above. Many of us discount the reality that all of our lives are interconnected, so rather than try to view our lives as having a more significant purpose than just work, family, and friends, we choose to accept defeat and ignore our desires for something more. Have you ever found yourself saying, "It's not like I can change the world or anything, right?"?

This book is written predominantly for men. Most of the men I know don't have time to sit and read anything for any period of time. Most don't have time to play with their kids as much as they would like. Most of the men I know won't take time to sit and read a book until it is late at night after the kids are asleep, the chores are done, and so on, and at that point we are lucky if we can stay awake long enough to get past three or four pages. Dedicated, driven, hardworking men like things short and simple—just get to the point and let me get on with what I need to do.

Men are more logic oriented. We don't generally base our decisions on feelings and emotions. Even so, as much as we try to stifle our feelings, even the toughest men will still feel and love and hurt and worry as much as women do. At the same time, we know what needs to be done and do it in spite of how we feel. Oftentimes, men will not react to feelings, but that does not mean in any way that we don't have them.

Generally, people don't like to be told what to do; I certainly don't like it when I am told what to think or feel. The direction my life has taken may not be the same direction yours has. Your experiences will be different than mine, but we all search for answers to life's questions. This book is not written with the intent to tell you what to think. Rather, the purpose is to ask you questions and provoke you to think for yourself—to get you to think about your life and your purpose from what may be a slightly different angle than how you were taught to think about life before.

As you read, search deep inside yourself and face your fears. Freedom is not the result of having nothing to fear; freedom comes from facing your fears. How does any man or woman find true happiness? How do we find true love? The answers are very simple. However, the process can be very difficult for many. If you are willing to give up what you thought was important, you can find true love and happiness. And at the same time, you can change the world.

THE QUESTIONS WE ALL ASK

EVERY ONE OF US HAS asked the questions "Why am I alive? What is the purpose of life?" At some point in life each of us has stood in front of a mirror and contemplated how it was possible to see our reflection, staring at ourselves with an almost surreal feeling like we were watching a movie in a theater.

Maybe you were in your kitchen. You went to open a cupboard to pull out a glass when suddenly, you realized all of the motions that needed to happen did so automatically just because you thought of the glass. How is this possible? There is almost a sense of discomfort that comes with not really being sure how all this works, a desire to understand how life and thought are even possible. All of us look for the answers to life's great mysteries in many ways. Yet, at the same time, there is always a fear of finding the truth.

When we can't find the answers or don't like what we hear, we discount it and just spend our lives looking for whatever pleasures make us feel good in the moment. The pleasures of life distract us—for a period of time. Eventually, all of us face tragedies of some sort that bring us back to the search for understanding. If nothing else, we face old age, when the usual pleasures don't bring pleasure anymore or we just can no longer participate. Any man or woman who has ever lost a limb will tell you how much we take the simple things for granted.

Each of us has our own unique set of experiences in life, and the challenges we face shape our own unique set of questions. We tend to look for answers from the people who are most important to us. You may have loved ones, family, friends, or mentors who have given you their perspective on the mysteries of life. You may have a religious background, a belief in a higher power of some sort that establishes your understanding of life. Either way, you will still ask many of these same questions. Write down some of your own if you don't see them in the list below.

Where did I come from?

Why do I feel empty inside?

Why do I feel like I'm missing something?

Why don't I feel happy?

Why don't I feel peace?

What will happen to me when I die?

Is there a God?

If there is, does He hear me?

The answer any particular person may give to one of these questions is based purely on their perspective of life. Many believe the answers are subjective, based on whatever that particular person's opinion is. At the same time, any person's opinions on life and the purpose thereof is based on a belief in something that cannot be seen or touched: faith.

You could read a hundred biology textbooks to learn about how the human body works. Scientists around the world are finding new cures for cancer every day, yet they still don't seem to know exactly what causes many types of cancer. If you look for information on what causes cancer, you will find that the list seems to include just about everything. Even things that we know are good, even essential, for our bodies in small amounts can be destructive in large amounts. For all our collective scientific knowledge around the world, scientists know how the brain sends messages yet we still don't know how thoughts, memories, and emotions are actually possible.

The ultimate debate of how life originated is the intellectual battle between creationism and evolution. Evolution says that over millions of years, all life on Earth came to be because of millions of random events that just happened to occur in the right order. Basically, all life is just one huge accident. No matter how much of an atheist you may be, it is still very difficult for anyone to believe that all life on Earth as we know it is the result of one giant accident. That is why channels like *The Discovery Channel* and *The Science Channel* are so popular—all of us have an inherent desire to learn about the incredible world around us.

We also all possess a level of faith that shows itself in a variety of ways. Faith is the belief in something that we don't have physical or logical proof of. We have faith that the driver next to us will follow the rules of the road as we do. Yet, accidents happen all the time because people fall asleep at the wheel, drive under the influence, or simply don't pay attention. We have faith that our local grocery store will always have food, yet during the pandemic scares of recent years, many national security experts estimated that the nation would lose close to 40 percent of our truck drivers due to severe illness. That shift alone could result in many grocery stores running out of food.

When you love someone, you have faith that they love you as well. When we are young, we often think that faith comes from how we feel, a burst of emotion that makes us believe something is real. Young love is one powerful example. Consider the teenage boy who falls head over heels for the first young girl who seems to like him. He has faith that she feels the same way, yet as almost all of us have found at some point, this love is often a short-term thing or is one-sided.

She may like him, but not nearly as much as he likes her. Even though she didn't intend to hurt him, his heart is then shattered, and his ability to have faith in the love of the next girl is diminished just a little. No one is perfect; even the people you love the most will hurt you at some point. Probably not intentionally, but it will happen. Any love given or received requires faith. If your faith cannot reach beyond the limitations of other people, with all their human faults and flaws, you will never experience real love.

Every religion on Earth, as its ultimate end or perfection, has this principle of faith, the ability to completely trust in something that is guiding your life, your day-to-day activities, the ultimate end or destiny. This is the understanding that something other than you is in control of your life. As I grow older, I realize more and more that much of life is beyond my direct control.

Some religions require you to have faith in a higher power, a God that directs and controls your life. You can't tell whether God is real or not based on your physical senses; instead, you make a decision to believe in your heart and soul that you know He is real. This faith may be based on an experience in life you can't explain, or it may be the result of a direction your life took without your influence or some type of miracle that impacted your life in such a way that you can only attribute it to a higher unseen power. Some say it is purely chance or luck. Their belief is that life is just a series of random, unplanned events. Those who attempt to believe this are often left with so many more questions than answers. They often spend a lifetime feeling lost.

We are emotional beings. We need to give and receive love. In fact, we usually search for it all our lives. So many of us go through life making decisions based on how we feel rather than what we know is true. Again, love requires faith. The result is a common theme that runs through our present-day society. We desire to know the truth, but at the same time we can't muster up the faith to believe it unless we have some physical, tangible proof.

We follow this same principle in other areas of our lives as well, one being religion. We know we need to have faith in something unseen in order to find peace and understanding of life's greatest mysteries, but we aren't able to truly believe unless we see some type of physical evidence to prove it is real. All of us experience things in life that prove God is real, but often we choose to discount them as something other than proof of God. We choose to believe things *just happen.*

It is just too inconvenient to have faith in God, because if He is real, then we think we have to follow someone else's rules rather than our own. Once you accept the idea that God is real, you have a responsibility to act accordingly. You inherently know that you need to follow His "rules." If you accept that God is real, you most certainly must accept that the devil is real as well. In the process, the devil tries to use this against you to make you feel guilty and ashamed every time you do something wrong. This creates discouragement. As a result, many people lose their faith in God because they do not understand His simple message of love and forgiveness.

Throughout the ages, men have screwed up what God was trying to do because our own selfish desires created a flawed interpretation of what He actually intended. The result of this inherently imperfect process is organized religion, a great many rules and requirements created by man's skewed version of His simple message. These rules are required to provide structure and keep men from falling to their own devices, but I don't believe God ever intended for us to make Him this complex. These rules prevent us from understanding the true meaning of God's purpose and love for us. Despite the muddled nature of organized religion, there are also times that something so significant happens that we can't help but believe.

When I was about twelve, I was playing with some friends outside their house. I felt a sting on the back of my leg and looked and saw a small bee. I brushed it off and tried to pick at the spot to pull out the stinger. After playing for a while, I noticed some bumps on my arms and started getting really hot. By the time we got to the hospital, I was having trouble breathing. I already had allergies to dust and went to a clinic every week for an injection, and now the doctors were telling me I was going to have to carry around a small first aid kit with a bee sting antidote. Basically, if I ever got a bee sting again, I was going to have to give myself an injection or die.

A few months later I was at a church. As I contemplated the torment of walking through life carrying a syringe in my pocket, I asked the pastor to pray for my allergies. Later, I returned to the allergy clinic for another round of painful allergy testing injections (for those of you who have had them, you know what I mean). When we got the tests back, everything was negative! Not just for bee stings, but for dust allergies as well.

Years later, I ended up spending a considerable part of my life working in construction. For a couple of years I was in a different person's home every day pulling out an old furnace or air conditioner so I could install a new one. Some were old oil furnaces that belched clouds of soot as you took them apart. Unsurprisingly, clouds of dust will cause anyone lung problems. I'd breathed in more dust than my share, but I didn't really have any more problems than anyone else.

I have experienced bee stings on a number of occasions after that incident with no adverse reaction. One time in particular, I was installing an air conditioner in a house in a cul-de-sac. I wheeled the condenser—the big box that sits outside the house—around to the back and set it on the ground next to where the unit was supposed to go, then I went back to my van to grab the concrete slab the unit sits on. It was supposed to sit off the back of the garage, where a pedestrian door connected the garage to the backyard. I noticed a small hole under the concrete slab by the door but didn't think anything of it. I scraped a little of the grass off to make the dirt level and as I was doing this, I noticed a bumblebee fly around me and into the hole. Again, I didn't think much of it. I lined up the pad and let it drop on the ground in place. It landed exactly where I wanted but dropped with a huge thud.

Within a split second, hundreds of bumblebees poured out of that tiny hole in the dirt and bombarded me. I ran as fast as I could, throwing my arms everywhere, spinning and dancing around as I ran. I ran past my van and down the middle of the street past a dozen or so houses, at least half a block, before I ditched all of them. I know I killed a few of them, but I was stung three times in the process. Just one sting could have been life-threatening for me if it were not for the miraculous healing I experienced. Nothing happened to me. I went to the store afterwards, bought a couple cans of bug killer, and sprayed all of it in the hole. After taking a short break, I was able to continue with the installation without any problems. A couple of bees were still buzzing around, but they didn't bother me.

I have shared that story many times over the years. Some have tried to say that I just outgrew my allergies or that my body just naturally changed somehow as I grew older. This is scientifically unlikely, but even if this were true, it would still be a miracle. To be honest, I find it comforting to believe that something miraculous happened to me rather than something accidental.

True faith cannot be dependent on some sort of physical evidence. A toddler has faith in the love of parents. Yes, parents give affection, quality time, food, shelter, clothing, and toys. These are expressions or evidence of love, yet there is still an element of faith the child holds on to. When the child does something wrong or wants something that they should not have, parents have to say no, correct the behavior, or discipline the child. When parents do this correctly, the child's "faith" in the love of their parents allows the child to develop the understanding that there must be a reason for Mom, Dad, or Uncle Joe to say no. All too often, we experience pains or fear as children that corrupt our faith in the love of those around us. This corrupts our ability to have faith in love as adults, leading to relationship problems that last a lifetime.

For those who have experienced combat, violent crime, multiple casualty traffic accidents, house fires, or similar horrific events, there is an additional set of questions we ask. The following is a list of these. Again, please write down some of your own questions if they are not represented here. Maybe there is a specific incident that left you at a loss of understanding, something so horrific or tragic that you were left with a burning sense of "Why, God?!"

Why do men kill each other?

Why do people hate each other?

Why doesn't He protect innocent people from violence and pain?

Why doesn't He save innocent children from abuse, torture, and rape?

Why doesn't He save children from starvation in third-world countries?

If there is a God, why does He let men do this to each other?

How could an all-powerful God with unconditional love for all men allow a father to physically, sexually, or emotionally abuse his own child?

Why did God take my son, my daughter, my wife?

Why did I survive when so many others did not?

All of us are affected by tragedies that occur in our lives or the lives of those around us. It may be violence that you experienced, someone close to you experienced, or something that happened to a stranger. A very small percentage of us have observed firsthand the worst humanity has to offer.

Some have charged into the closest thing to hell on Earth and survived, watched friends get cut into pieces on either side as ear-shattering explosions threw them to the ground. Maybe you were the first soldier to walk into an abandoned torture chamber, or the first cop to find the body of a kidnapped, abused, and murdered child. Maybe you are an EMT who responded to what was left of a family of five hit head-on by a drunk driver. You held a broken, bleeding child in your arms knowing there was nothing you could do while life slowly slipped away and the small body went limp. I could detail a hundred different incidents that could literally be described as hell on Earth. Something different happens to these folks who face this firsthand every day.

The saying "There are no atheists in foxholes" comes to mind. No matter what you believed before, the man in the middle of a combat zone, seeing others die next to him while bullets whiz by his head, will call out to God for help and protection, often without even realizing it. After the battle is over, we remember those who have fallen. The man who survived feels guilt because he is alive when so many of his fellow soldiers are dead. Anger wells up within. There is no one to blame for the loss, the guilt, and the anger except God.

We start to question why these things happen. We go to church to hear about the love of God and all the miracles Jesus did. During Christmas and Easter, we are constantly reminded of His death for us on a cross to save us from our sins. We hear about creation, how powerful He is, and, again, His love for us. Then we see the cruelty that men display to each other, or we see the cruelty some men display to women and children. We question how a God so powerful could allow people to hurt each other so much.

A God who created the entire Earth and everything in it could stop this. A God who loves all of us so much that He died to save us wouldn't let people do this. We think to ourselves, "If I had even a fraction of that kind of power, I would make sure no one was ever able to do such a thing!" Our ability, or even our desire, to believe in such a God is shaken. We are cut to the very core of our heart because we can't imagine how such a reality could be possible. We want to understand. We want to believe that there is a reason for God to allow such cruelty and suffering, but we can't imagine why. We shout at the sky and demand answers. So often, we don't hear the answers we are looking for.

Or do we?

WHY, GOD?!

As a child, I wasn't very active. I was overweight. I didn't have a lot of friends. My parents weren't really interested in sports, fishing, hunting, camping, and so on. Consequently, I was the kid that got picked on and beat up a lot. I never had anyone who could teach me how to stand up for myself. I was really miserable as a child. My parents loved me, and there were a lot of people around me who cared about me, but even the couple of friends I had as a child often gave into peer pressure and picked on me along with the other kids. Even though childhood was miserable, I held on to the belief that God had something better for me in the future. I heard a number of preachers say, "You know God has something big planned for you when the devil starts attacking you." That is exactly how my childhood felt—like one constant attack. I would randomly get beat up by groups of kids on a regular basis, and at times I wished I had never been born. I really hated life and most of the time I felt like I was basically all alone. I kept praying and asking God why I got beat up and teased all the time. It seemed like he wasn't listening, because it never stopped.

When I was about thirteen, some friends told us about a youth camp their son went to. I went to the camp a couple years in a row and started attending the youth group at the church that was affiliated with the camp. There, I met Paris Pasch. Paris was the youth pastor at that church and was also in charge of the camp. An iron worker by trade, he designed and created custom staircases, fountains, sculptures, etc. He was strong and tough, but he also had incredible compassion and wisdom. He was the first "Christian" man I'd ever met who didn't seem like a weenie. (I had the opportunity to meet George Foreman, the boxer and grill guy, at camp one year—also not a weenie.) When trouble comes your way, you need to pray. Unlike any other preacher I had ever heard, he also told us he would fight with every ounce of energy he had in his body if anyone ever broke into his house to hurt his wife or kids. He wasn't just going to jump into the closet to start praying. He would fight, and he meant it.

Paris made an impression on me right from the start. I enjoyed spending time with him and his family. To this day, I am proud to call him my friend, but it was something he did when we first met that literally turned my life around. Our youth group went on a ski trip. I liked to ski, but at that point in my life I wasn't very good at it and I wasn't very athletic, either, so I spent most of the trip skiing by myself. There were only a couple other kids in the youth group I would consider friends, but they were much better skiers than me. They were off on the more difficult runs most of the time, or passing me on the runs I was able to ski. At one point, I took a wrong turn and ended up at the top of one of the more difficult runs. Oddly enough, Paris happened to show up at that very moment. He kept encouraging me that I could do it. He told me we would ski it together. If I fell behind, he would wait for me at the bottom.

We started down the hill, but I couldn't control my speed. I was going too fast. I got scared, lost my balance, and fell over just a few feet down the hill. Paris got to the bottom and yelled, "Are you OK?" I replied that I was fine. I was too unsure of myself to ski the rest of the way down; I could barely stand up to get the skis on as it was. I put my skis on my shoulder and started walking down the hill. He told me I could do it. I told him to just keep going, that I would catch up with him later, but nope—he'd said he would wait, and he was going to wait.

I kept waiving to Paris to just go ahead and ski, but he stayed there.

When I finally got to the bottom of the hill, he again asked if I was OK. He told me everyone gets scared a little sometimes and that it was nothing to be ashamed of. "Keep practicing and the next time that hill will seem like nothing!" He asked where I wanted to ski next. I thanked him for waiting, but I decided I wanted to go inside and warm up a little. He repeated his encouraging words and then went on his way to find out how everyone else was doing.

Parents are supposed to love you. Parents are supposed to wait for you at the bottom of the hill. Grandparents are supposed to love you. For all children, it is important for them to know that their parents love them and care about how they feel, but that really isn't the same as knowing someone, other than a relative, genuinely cares. Paris had a bunch of kids to keep an eye on. I don't think for a moment that he cared about me more than any other kid in the youth group, yet he cared enough about me to stand at the bottom of a ski hill for several minutes to make sure I was OK and make sure I didn't feel bad about walking down the hill. He didn't have to do that, but he did. He cared enough about me specifically to wait.

This may seem like an insignificant event to many, but it had an incredibly profound effect on my life. Again, I knew he would do the same thing for anyone else, but the fact that he had wasted time, taken the time, waiting for me meant a lot. However small anyone may think this is, this was one of the first times I saw God's love for me through another person. In all reality, Paris was very much a stranger to me at the time. I was just one of many kids in the youth group. Even so, he cared deeply about all the kids in his youth group.

Something changed inside me after experiencing this love. I made a commitment to exercise and work out. Life changed drastically, and it only got better and better over the years. I have often wondered how such a brief moment in life could have such a huge impact. We can waste a great deal of time in life asking how or why, but the fact of the matter is, it did. There are times when a small show of kindness and love can have a huge life-changing impact on someone's life, especially in the life of a child or teenager. Don't miss out on the chance to change someone's life.

I graduated high school from a small Christian school. My graduating class was a total of eight people. Every time I tell someone this, I get the same joke: "At least you can say you graduated in the top ten!" Ha, ha. My family was one of several who had kids enrolled in the school but lived in a different town, so we carpooled together. The moms or dads would alternate days.

One of the moms we carpooled with was an enthusiastic Christian woman, the mother of two of the kids I went to school with. She always seemed in a good mood and was the kind of person who always remained upbeat. She would talk about how great God was and how much He had done for her. She would sing along with the songs on the radio. She seemed truly confident in life and God, to the point of being annoying to her kids and the rest of us "cool" kids. She always seemed truly happy. If I remember correctly, we carpooled with them for about a year.

One day, we were out playing soccer on the playground when the principal came outside and brought her two kids inside. When the rest of us came inside, we were told that their father had come home earlier that day and shot their mom several times. This lady we had carpooled with was dead. I never knew much of the events leading up to that point, but we heard that he had been very abusive for a long time. He was convicted and went to jail. A few months later, a couple of pastors went to see him in jail. We heard that he was sorry for what he had done and turned his life over to God.

The kids went to live with relatives, and we didn't really see them after that. For years I wondered how God could let this happen. This didn't just affect her—her kids were now left without a mother or father. What happened to the phrases I had heard in church for years? "The weapons of our warfare are not carnal," "The battle belongs to the Lord," and so on. Did she give her life to save her husband's life? Over the years I have heard of similar tragedies. Anyone close to the family always has the same questions. Most of them come down to this.

Why does God allow bad things to happen to good people?

We all worry about things in life. We worry about someone breaking into our home, hurricanes, tornadoes, kidnapping, house fires, gas leaks, and other disastrous events. We hear about crime on the news. It used to be that was all we had to worry about. For decades, it was the Cold War. We worried about whether someone was going to accidentally push the button that would launch all the nuclear weapons in the world. Now, we hear about terrorism striking from across the globe. Anthrax, Smallpox, Sarin gas, and suicide bombers have become common day-to-day terms.

Before September 11, 2001, you were more likely to be struck by lightning than be killed in a terrorist attack. That is not the case anymore. This is, of course, based on statistics. The fact that so many people were killed because of one event creates a statistical probability. Dozens of people are killed by lightning each year, but one event can greatly change the statistics.

National security and terrorism experts had warned of such an attack for years. I still have the magazine articles from the first World Trade Center bombing naming Bin Laden as the man who orchestrated it. The overwhelming response these national security experts received for years was typical of the average American attitude. Even when provided with evidence, the response from the public and politicians was, "Oh, that will never happen here."

It doesn't matter whether tragedy is the result of a lightning strike, car accident, house fire, or terrorist attack. Someone could try to stab you and take your car, or you could fall from a ladder onto a grounding rod. If you are the victim of harm, the statistics don't matter anymore. All of us need to take the time to be aware of our surroundings. Each of us has a responsibility to make sure we can go home to our families each night. We need to train ourselves to be aware of crime and disaster rather than fall into the fatal trap of believing "It probably won't happen to me anyway."

It is all too easy to get caught up in the daily routine of life, often creating false confidence for ourselves that we almost always know where we will be at any given time on any given day. We make and follow schedules. We plan ahead for events. Life is based on the plans that we make and the anticipation that those plans will not change, and so many of us develop a false sense of faith in the plans we make. If for some reason something alters our plans (someone is late, the weather doesn't cooperate, sickness, etc.), it is tragic. The agony of having to reschedule and reorganize plans is just too much to bear!

This becomes the worst thing in life until real tragedy hits. A husband doesn't come home from work one day. He is killed in a car accident. Now, suddenly, all of our schedules, plans, and dreams for the future are shattered, permanently. Everything we believed in or had faith in is gone. This destruction of our faith in life compounds the pain of losing a loved one.

When tragic and terrible things happen, some of us spend a lifetime searching for the answer to this one simple question: Why? Why did this have to happen? None of us like to relive bad memories or horrific experiences, but I would encourage you to think back to the events that have changed your life. Think about the questions you were left with but never found answers for. Even if your experiences seem minor compared to a truly horrific experience someone else has had, still write them down. If you don't, they will torment you forever.

So, how do we answer these questions? I have read dozens of quotes from famous people who all say the same thing: Don't waste today thinking about yesterday. How do we deal with these feelings so we don't spend our lives missing the enjoyment of the present because we are wondering about the past? This is easier said than done, but we must search for peace. Until you can make peace with the past, you will never find peace in the present.

SACRIFICE! WHAT'S IN IT FOR ME?

THIS BOOK IS DEDICATED TO Arnold Riemer Sr., my grandfather, a member of the Greatest Generation. He was born in May 1921 and died in February 2001 from a number of medical problems, primarily related to his lungs. My grandfather worked in factories for years, constantly breathing in a lot of dust and contaminants. He worked hard all his life, sacrificing himself for the good of his family.

The last few years of his life, he couldn't walk more than a few yards before having to stop and catch his breath. I didn't have the opportunity to spend much time with him. As teenagers, we have dreams and ambitions that create a desire to get away from family and experience life; I didn't appreciate the time I had with him when I was younger. A decade or so later, I still didn't have the opportunity to spend much time with him, but I began to appreciate that time so much more.

My grandfather served in WWII. I always knew this but never really knew much about it, and he never talked about it. If someone brought up the subject, he would very casually change the subject. There really wasn't much emotion displayed; he just didn't really want to talk about it. He always reminded me a lot of John Wayne. A number of years ago, my parents found a life-size cardboard cutout of John Wayne, and I still have the cutout and pictures of my grandfather standing next to it with his arm around it.

He was tough but a kind-hearted and loving man. My grandmother, Marjorie, died of cancer when I was in elementary school. A number of years later, he fell in love again. Betty and Arnold were together until he died. He loved, worked hard, and sacrificed for years. I guess I never really appreciated the courage he had until after he died. When he passed away, Betty received the flag. After talking with my mom, they sent the flag to me along with his medals and related papers.

On his honorable discharge paper, it lists his civilian occupation as FURNACE TENDER 4-91.511. Having worked in the heating and cooling industry for many years taking apart old furnaces, I now realize one of the reasons why he had such problems with his lungs later in life. I can't imagine the dust and soot he must have sucked in over the years. When he was in his prime, there weren't many safety regulations related to air quality. His military occupation was listed as RIFLEMAN 745. He had received a Victory Medal, Overseas Service Bars, a Good Conduct Medal, and a Bronze Star. Along with this was a letter from the War Department. It reads:

CITATION
AWARD OF THE BRONZE STAR MEDAL
By direction of the President, under the provisions of
Army Regulations, the Bronze Star is awarded to:
ARNOLD H. RIEMER
Private First Class, Infantry, Company C, 222nd Infantry, for meritorious achievement in action on January 12, 1945, near Ingolsheim, France.

While on a combat patrol deep into enemy territory near Ingolsheim, France, Private Riemer unhesitatingly advanced ahead of his patrol to neutralize an approaching vehicle with his bazooka. Fearlessly moving ahead, he fired one round and destroyed the vehicle, wounding the two occupants. Later, when the patrol was pinned down by enemy small arms fire, he exposed himself again to direct accurate fire into the enemy positions, neutralizing them and enabling his comrades to escape without casualty. Private Riemer's courageous action and unswerving devotion to duty played a major role in the successful accomplishment of the patrol's mission.

HARRY J. COLLIN
Major General, USA, Commanding

Reading this for the first time, I was excited and proud. No one in the family had ever told me anything about medals he received; I'd had no knowledge of his heroic efforts. After thinking about this, I started to wonder. Why wouldn't a man of such courage be proud of this and be happy to talk about it? Did thinking about the event bring back unbearable memories? Was he tormented by having killed other men? From the brief description I have of the event, it sounds like he went forward by himself and took out the enemy vehicle before they even knew the Americans were there. I also have a brief newspaper article that states he "stood up" under heavy enemy fire to direct fire from his patrol against enemy positions. The letter of commendation states this all happened behind enemy lines.

I assume there were other firefights he lived through, situations of equal danger that were never recognized. The letter said there were no American casualties in this particular event, but I can imagine there were other times this was not the case. Did the thought (or any thought) of combat bring up the worst memories of seeing his friends die around him?

Some veterans feel guilt because they survived and others didn't. Others are eternally grateful just to be alive. I wonder if he felt his courage was more of an overwhelming fear that had just grabbed hold of him and pushed him to react without even thinking. When threatened, every person will have an automatic response that just takes over and pushes us to do something without even really processing what is going on.

Maybe it wasn't guilt. Maybe it was a feeling of helplessness. When he was faced with an overwhelming threat, did he feel like his actions suddenly went out of control? Did his fight-or-flight reaction force him to do things he would never normally do? Was he concerned it could happen again? I don't know the answers to these questions; I don't know how he felt. Everything happens for a reason. All men make their individual choices, and every choice we make plays an important role in the larger picture of how life unfolds for all of us. Every choice we make has an impact on others around us.

His courage in one event may have led to saving the life of one of his fellow soldiers who was to go on to invent something that benefits all of us. This one small event behind enemy lines may have had an impact on enemy soldiers or leadership, altering the course of the war. His courage may have inspired one of his fellow soldiers to be courageous in a later battle, saving the lives of countless others.

There are so many possible reasons for the events of that day, or any other battle he was involved in. At times, we are forced into situations in life that require us to react to a threat of harm to ourselves or others. His responsibility as a soldier and American at that time was to follow the orders of his commanders and do everything in his power to survive so he could come home to be a father and husband. That was his only responsibility.

Yes, the men who died as a result were just ordinary men like him from the enemy side. The term "enemy" is used to harden men and reduce the guilt felt when a soldier kills another human being. Every soldier I have met struggles with this. Every man in that battle—American or German, friend or enemy, attacker of defender—who carried a weapon into battle was responsible for his own destiny. Whether you die in combat or get hit by a truck a block from home, every man must be ready to live for a purpose and eventually die for the same. Every man chooses his purpose. Every man decides his own fate.

The only way to really live life to the fullest and die with peace is to have a belief in something greater than ourselves. Martin Luther King Jr. said, "If a man hasn't discovered something that he will die for, he isn't fit to live" (23 June 1963, Detroit, Mich.). This is a never-ending dedication to act and react when we, our loved ones, or our way of life is threatened, whether the threat is at the front door or from the other side of the ocean. The confidence to act correctly comes from the core principles of freedom and justice for all. Our constitutionally recognized God-given rights, our core values, are ingrained in us through our faith. This is what we live for, fight for, and eventually die for.

Every man from everywhere in the world must also determine for himself what is right. What is important to him and his loved ones? What he will fight and die for? A man on the other side of the battlefield may determine that it is important is to destroy what you hold dear. His leaders may have decided this for him. You have no control over the decisions that man makes or whether he has made peace with God; all you can do is fight for what you believe is right. After that, the outcome of who wins the battle is in God's hands, along with the life or death of every soldier on either side. Even if the enemy soldier was forced to fight by his leaders, his individual destiny is not something you can be responsible for. His will to fight or die and his individual peace with God is not something you have control over.

A lot of Americans struggle with the idea of why we send our young men and women into battle on the other side of the world. Every American soldier volunteers to serve. Our core principles say that every person—not just Americans, but every person—has the God-given right to life, liberty, and the pursuit of happiness.

No government on Earth can protect your freedoms. There are only two things the government can do: it can take your freedoms from you, or it can act after your freedoms have already been taken away. It is every citizen's responsibility to make sure no one infringes on another person's inherent rights.

We cannot believe in these principles unless we also believe that the principles apply to everyone, everywhere. This is why churches send missionaries around the world. The Red Cross and other organizations send doctors, scientists, and construction workers to all corners of the globe. When disaster strikes, America leads the world in sending people and supplies to help.

We have ingrained in us the desire to help those who cannot help themselves, to protect those who cannot protect themselves. Americans want others to have the same opportunities we have. When America was born, we were fighting for our own freedom from an enemy on the other side of the world. Our principles of freedom drive us to stand up and fight for others the way so many fought with us when America was new.

We see these principles reflected in the Middle East today. Over the last several years, citizens in Iraq, Afghanistan, Iran, Libya, Syria, and Egypt have worked together to stand up and fight against oppressive dictators. Our actions in Iraq and Afghanistan have helped the people in other countries see that they can fight for freedom. Are these wars bloody? Yes. Does it turn our stomachs as we watch the news to see cities on fire and hear that hundreds of people died in the fighting today? Yes. Our own history shows that we know our freedom is never free.

Just as we know there will always be good people in the world, we also know there will always be bad people. We could spend a lifetime debating why this is, but the fact of the matter is that it's true. There will always be people fighting each other, but we love a good fight. The Olympic Games started as a way for opposing nations to stop killing each other and settle their differences by competing in games of sports—a fair fight. We enjoy watching boxing, wrestling, football, and hockey for this reason.

All men throughout the world have an inherent desire to compete. In foreign lands, the popular sports are rugby and soccer. Individual sports are enjoyed throughout the world as well, and millions of people throughout the world participate in martial arts competitions. It is important for men and women to compete, as conflict, struggles, and competition allow us to grow. This is how we learn to endure hardships. Competition is how we push each other to be better.

When we see a man get shoved to the ground by a bully, we stand up and push the bully back. Then, we stretch out a hand and help the man stand up, and when he is ready to fight back, we charge into battle alongside him. If nothing else, we stand behind him to help make sure the fight is fair. This is why we send our military to all corners of the globe. Any nation throughout history that appreciated freedom knew men would always desire to fight for what they believe is right, but we want to see a fair fight.

Our core beliefs push us to reach out and help level the playing field. Americans know that the only way we can insure our own rights and freedoms is to help others fight for their rights and freedoms as well. We cannot forget those men and women who have given their lives doing so.

THE HOME FRONT

WHAT IF YOU HAVE NEVER served in the military? What about the men and women who aren't soldiers, cops, or firemen? What can we do? What can *I* do? Am I just out of luck or off the hook, depending on how you look at it? Do the rest of us just sit back and enjoy? Is it enough to just be thankful for what others have done? In a way, yes, we can all be thankful for our freedoms and enjoy life because of the sacrifices others have made. At the same time, we have our own battles going on here in our own neighborhoods every day.

Teenagers all over the country seek out and find help and protection in street gangs because they can't find it at home from their own parents. A large portion of the last several generations has no understanding of what it is like to be part of a loving family, as their parents were never around for a variety of reasons. Some were intoxicated all the time, and others were at work from the moment the kids woke up to the moment they were picked up from day care at their bedtime.

Some of these children have no self-worth because they never received any attention from their parents. For others, the only attention they ever received was physical, emotional, or sexual abuse. The love of our parents is the most important element of healthy human development. When this is destroyed, we begin to destroy our nation's very foundation. The love for our family is the heart of what drives our desire to work hard, serve others, and respect each other's rights. How do we make this important again? We start by changing the way we view each other.

We have been raised to depend on police, firefighters, and paramedics and to expect they will always be there when we call. In rural Minnesota, much of local law enforcement is just the county sheriff. Depending on the time of day, you may have only a couple of deputies driving around an entire county. Depending on their location and what is going on at the time, it could be five minutes before a deputy can get to you if you call 911. It could be much longer. A lot can happen in five minutes. Almost all of our local fire response team is made up of volunteers. They don't sit at the fire station and wait for a call; they carry pagers while they are at work and home. When someone needs help, they drop everything, drive to the local fire station, throw on their turnout gear, and jump into a truck.

These men and women are dedicated. They take great risks just getting to a burning home as fast as they can, never mind the risk of running into a burning building to pull you out. As with the sheriff's deputies, even moving as fast as they can, it may take the volunteer fire department six, eight, or ten minutes to get to you if you call for help. To make matters worse, there are no fire hydrants out here in farm country. Almost every call requires regular fire trucks as well as a tanker truck carrying thousands of gallons of water. As citizens, so many of us just assume that we can call 911 and wait for help. The fact of the matter, though, is that crime, especially violent crime, happens in less than a minute. The only way for us to truly, completely depend on law enforcement to protect everyone from all crime would be for every man, woman, and child to have their own cop.

Every person and every family has a responsibility for their own safety. There are simple things you can do: Make sure you have a couple of fire extinguishers in your home, even in your vehicles. Make sure every room in your home has a smoke detector and CO detector. Every adult should take a basic CPR and first aid class. Take a self-defense course.

Look around your home. Do you have the best doors and locks you can get? Do you have fire escape ladders in your second-floor bedrooms? Talk with your kids so they know what to do if there is an emergency. Teach them how to get out of the house, how to call for help, and where they should go.

No one wants to talk about violence. We watch it constantly in movies and on TV, but this seems to create a disconnect or desensitization in our minds. People don't seem to realistically grasp that the horrible things we watch for entertainment could and do happen to people. It could very well happen to you, too—but most people would prefer not to think about this. If you don't talk with your kids and prepare your family for disaster, you really have no way to know if they will respond correctly. We run fire and tornado drills in schools all over the nation, and now we even run active shooter drills in schools. This doesn't scare children; it helps them be ready for the real thing.

What will you do if tragedy strikes your home, your family? Do you have a fire extinguisher in the house? Do you know how to use it? There are times when a kitchen fire rages out of control in spite of your best effort to put it out. The fire may destroy your kitchen, but your efforts with a fire extinguisher before the fire department gets there could keep it from destroying your entire home. There will always be emergencies that grow beyond your control, and this is where our public safety services step in to help.

There is no question that we need the best law enforcement, fire, and EMS programs in our communities, but each citizen also has a responsibility to be ready for the worst life can throw at us. No matter how experienced you are, no matter how well trained you are, any individual can only fight for so long. A well-trained cop may be able to fight off two street thugs for a short period of time, but his energy will only last for a few minutes. He needs help as soon as possible, not just from his fellow officers but from any good citizen who happens to be close. Public safety personnel depend on us as much as we depend on them.

Each of us will deal with crime at some point. If you have ever had your car broken into or stolen, you know the accompanying feeling of helplessness. We depend on the police to respond and do whatever they can to find the criminal and get our property back. Sometimes they can; sometimes they can't. When I was younger, I had a 1988 Chevrolet IROC-Z Camaro. It had everything—T-tops, a 350ci motor, a striking charcoal-gray color, power everything. At 70 mph on the interstate, I could take a cloverleaf exit ramp without even taking my foot off the gas. It was an awesome car.

Back then, I was working a series of short term security jobs. I was in my 20s, young, cocky, and out of control. The job I had at the time was in Minneapolis. The third day on the job, I parked the car at 08:00. At 10:00, I spun a camera past the parking lot and it was gone. I was heartbroken. There wasn't even any glass on the ground! I called the police right away and did everything I was supposed to do. It didn't matter; the car was long gone.

A couple of months later, I got a call from Minneapolis PD. The detective said, "Mr. Herrmann, we think we have your car. We are having an insurance expert run the VIN numbers. We will call you back as soon as we know something definite." A couple days later I got another call: "Mr. Herrmann, what we have is part of your car." It turned out someone had swapped out some of the parts. Whoever had it last had gotten into a high-speed chase with the police and crashed it into a couple of parked cars.

They told me the car was pretty beat up and asked me if I wanted it back. I had already taken care of insurance, so I said no. My dream is to someday have another car like it. Every once in a while I find one for sale, but I have never had the money at the right time. There aren't too many of them around anymore. Dreams are good to have, but at the same time, I really appreciate the memories I have. I am thankful I had the opportunity to own such a car when I was young. It was a lot of fun.

We depend on dedicated men and women in public safety to come to our aid. Even when we do the best we can in those first few minutes of an emergency, things sometimes grow beyond our control. This is when we need help from people who are trained to help. If a friend falls off a ladder and hits his head on a rock, what will you do? Would you know how to help? Furthermore, would you be capable of dealing with your fear and anxiety in the moment in order to think clearly? Even the most experienced people can make a bad situation worse when they let fear get in the way of their judgment.

Each of us should know some basic first aid skills, but we need trained emergency medical personnel to help someone with a serious head injury. We will always depend on specially trained public safety personnel to help us deal with emergencies, but they will always depend on us as well. They depend on us to make good decisions when they aren't there to help us.

Most of the time we serve our fellow man in simple ways, like holding the door for each other as you enter the mall or stopping by the side of the road to help someone change a tire or just call for help. It is a simple act of respect all men should show each other regardless of race, religion, skin color, or language. Your personal safety must always be a priority, but you can still help make a cell phone call for a guy stranded on the side of the road. You don't have to get out of your car; you may not even have to roll the window down more than a crack!

Generally, the most that you sacrifice is some time. You might be on your way to a meeting and you really can't be late. At the same time, if the person stranded on the side of the road were your daughter, wife, or son, wouldn't you want someone to take a couple of minutes to help them? Being stranded on the side of the road may seem like a fairly benign issue, but think of this from a personal safety perspective. A young woman stranded on the side of the road is vulnerable to theft, assault, or abduction. If you have lived someplace like Minnesota or Arizona for a period of time, you know personal safety can also have a lot to do with other factors like the weather.

A number of years ago, I was on my way to work one evening in one of the worst blizzards of the year. I had a Chevy Silverado 4x4. Other than having slightly oversized tires, my truck was stock. Learning how to drive in the winter time on snow and ice is just that: a learned skill that only comes with experience. And, of course, driving yourself into a ditch a few times. That day, I got on the interstate and noticed several cars, trucks, and tractor-trailers stuck on the side of the road. I had my hazard lights on and slowly drove past each vehicle, looking to see if anyone was inside. I stopped a couple of times. I mainly wanted to make sure no one was hurt. Almost everyone has a cell phone nowadays, so long as the people in the vehicle had a cell phone and no one was hurt, I moved on.

I came to a bright-blue VW Jetta sitting at the bottom of the center median. I got out and walked up to the vehicle. Again, this was pretty much the worst blizzard of the season. Inside was a young Asian woman who didn't speak any English with, if I remember right, six kids in the car. The kids ranged in age from being an infant to probably seven years old, and the youngest had nothing but a diaper on. There were a couple of light summer coats in the car and no car seats. A couple of the kids were crying, but they were all moving around. It didn't look like they were hurt.

I tried to communicate, but it just wasn't working. I called the state patrol and waited in my truck for about ten minutes. I checked on her a couple of times. The only thing I could understand was that she kept asking for a tow. The car was pretty much buried up to the doors in snow. If I remember correctly, I think I kicked some of the snow away from the exhaust pipe so she could keep the car running for the kids.

As severe as the storm was, I was surprised the state patrol made it there as quickly as they did. When the trooper arrived, I told him she was asking for a tow. He told me they wouldn't call for any tow trucks until the storm lightened up in a couple of hours; the roads were just too dangerous, even for the tow trucks. I helped him carry the woman and her kids, crying the whole time, up to his squad car. He just barely had enough room. He drove them to a truck stop where she could be warm, safe, and call for help. That's all they could do at the time. I didn't do much, but it was still important. I was late for work, as I had been before, but I would gladly do it again.

On a separate occasion, a storm had just rolled through and the roads were really icy. I was coming up on the exit I needed to take from the interstate into town and there was a tractor-trailer a few seconds ahead of me. Suddenly, a red late model F-350 crew cab pickup tried to cross in front of the tractor-trailer to get on the exit ramp. The pickup spun around 360 degrees about three times and hit the ditch nose first. There was quite a bit of snow in the ditches, and this guy hit the ditch so hard that snow and dirt were flying through the air. The impact with the ditch then threw the truck around another 180 degrees. By the time I slowed down enough to stop, I noticed the entire front end of the truck was crumpled and the windshield was completely blown out. His stuff that had been in the truck bed—tools, coolers, plastic totes, and other belongings—was now scattered everywhere through the ditch.

The driver got out of the truck. He was a Hispanic man from Texas—not much experience driving on ice, I was sure. He had a couple of cuts on his hands and his forehead. He didn't really look that bad. I remember he had one finger that was bent sideways. I asked him if that was normal, and he said yes, that finger injury had happened several years ago. His English was understandable, but you could tell he didn't get the chance to use it very often.

I drove him into a truck stop in town next to a hotel. I kept asking him if he wanted to go to the hospital, but he said no. I called the police to let them know what had happened and where he was. They were pretty busy at the time. He had a cell phone, so he told the police he would call for a tow himself. After I stayed with him for a little bit, he thanked me for the ride and I went to work, arriving late again.

Immigration and securing the borders are important issues. Diversity is the strength of our nation. People who come here from other countries appreciate their freedom; they understand how fragile it is. They bring with them a natural strength and desire to invest in the lives of others. Many of these folks seem much happier to be here than most native-born Americans. However, most people don't seem to take into account the public safety issues related to immigration. We have immigration laws and an established citizenship process for a reason. If you don't know the laws of the land and can't speak English enough to communicate with police and medical personnel, you shouldn't be able to get a driver's license.

There are times we sacrifice just our time or inconvenience to serve others, and then there are times we risk much more. For eight years we lived on a busy corner in South St. Paul, Minnesota. This was a four-way stop on one of the busiest streets in town. One summer day, I got into my truck with two of my kids to head down to the grocery store. I pulled out of our driveway onto the street and heard a lot of yelling. We would periodically hear yelling outside, people yelling at each other as they passed others walking or driving down the street. Sometimes it was serious, and other times it was just someone being obnoxious. I wasn't sure which situation this was yet.

I noticed a guy get out of a black pickup stopped at one corner. He was yelling at people in a tan car stopped at another corner of the four-way stop. As he started walking towards the car, I pulled up to the curb in front of my house. I was at the corner opposite where this was taking place. My kids were asking what was going on and I told them to sit down and stay in the back seat. I wrote down the license plate numbers of the truck and the car. I was going to call the police, but other than that, I was going to sit this one out.

I know how to take care of myself, and I know the law. At that point this was just a couple of idiots mouthing off to each other, disturbing the peace at most. But then another guy got out of the pickup and then two guys got out of the car. They started shoving each other around. I picked up my cell phone to call police when another green pickup pulled up to the curb across the street from where I was.

A middle-aged man with long hair got out of the green truck and walked up to the driver's side of the black pickup. He exchanged words with the driver for a moment and then tried to walk back to his truck. The driver of the black truck got out and started yelling at him, and soon he was joined by his buddies. They grabbed the driver of the green truck and started shoving him around. Anyone who has dealt with violent confrontations for a period of time seems to learn how to recognize when a situation has jumped from an unfriendly or hostile exchange of words to a violent encounter. I didn't know what the driver of the green pickup had said, but I knew this situation had jumped to the next level.

I shut my truck off and stuffed the key into my pocket, walked across the street, and pushed the biggest of the three guys away from the guy with the green truck. He took a swing at me. I blocked it, grabbed his arm, and spun him around. I had him in something of a modified armbar, and locked up his shoulder as we hit the ground. I kept yelling, "That's enough!" That's all that came to mind in the heat of the moment. As I locked up his arm, I looked across the street to see my wife running our kids into the house. She had been heading outside to get the kids about the same time I got out of the truck. About this time, we could hear police sirens and saw flashing lights coming down the street.

As I kept my guy locked up on the ground, I noticed one of his buddies heading toward me yelling to let him go. I was trying to think of how to keep control of the guy I already had and defend myself against the other guy as well. When he was almost on top of me, an angel appeared. I don't know if the guy was really an angel, but he was my saving grace at that moment. He grabbed the other thug by the shoulder and told him something.

I couldn't hear them even though both of them were standing almost right on top of me. I only caught a split second of the two of them standing there, and the "angel" had his arms up or he was pointing in a couple different directions. The thug took his advice. Instead of taking me on, he ran down an alley. The cops showed up. One grabbed the guy I was holding while another officer chased the second guy down the alley and tackled him. They took out someone's wooden privacy fence in the process.

After everyone was in custody, another car with a couple of guys showed up. It turns out the three guys in the black pickup were white supremacists on a drinking binge. They had driven by a house on the other side of town earlier and thrown a couple of glass bottles at two guys building a retaining wall. One of them was Hispanic. The guys in the tan car were Hispanic as well. The guys in the black truck started yelling at them when they stopped at the corner in front of my house.

If you are going to get involved in a violent situation, you really need to know what you can do, can't do, should do, and shouldn't do. The guy that had pulled up in the green truck was smaller than the guys in the black truck. He was also alone. He had walked up to the black truck to try to talk some sense into them, or something, and noticed the smell of alcohol on the young driver's breath and several empty beer bottles on the floor.

He had reached in, pulled the key out of the ignition, and started walking back to his truck. From what I remember, he told police he didn't want the intoxicated, angry, and emotional driver to run from the police. He might have ended up hurting himself or others. I commend the guy for stopping. He tried to make a difference in the interest of keeping people safe, but he took a huge risk in doing what he did. In the end, thankfully, no one was really hurt. After the police left, I got the kids and we finally went to the grocery store.

At times, the price we pay for standing up for what is right is not something immediate. As part of my job, I had been in a number of similar confrontations, but this was one of the first times I'd experienced something like that outside of work—and the first time it had happened right in front of my home. We never really had any problems with crime up to that day. After that incident, a couple of our vehicles were vandalized. Our garage was vandalized, and the motor was stolen right off my boat one Sunday morning while we were at church. But if you were to ask me if I would do it again, I would tell you, "Absolutely!"

Some of the most profound moments in our lives come from our sudden and unintended involvement in other people's tragedies, uncontrollable events that violently alter someone else's ability to live out a normal life. These are the types of events that shock our senses or confidence in life. Most people don't like to talk about death, crime, or other painful subjects, especially when we think of our loved ones. However, if you don't talk about it now, you won't be ready to deal with it when it happens.

When disaster strikes, we depend on so many people to come to our aid when tragedy strikes. Police, firemen, EMTs, National Guard members—they all risk their lives to help others. They sacrifice time with their families. They work for very little money, and they often drop everything at a moment's notice to answer a call for help. We take for granted that they will always be there when we call. We take for granted that these people have lives and dreams and families of their own as well. Why do they do it?

Some do it for the excitement, the so-called "adrenaline junkies" who just can't get enough of it. They relish the surge of energy combined with overwhelming fear as your senses tingle while walking through a building, firearm in hand, looking for who broke in, not knowing whether they are still inside someplace. Facing danger while walking the fine line between a controlled emergency and an out-of-control disaster is like a drug. There is an incredible surge of strength and speed, thoughts racing as you face a sudden threat. You see a flash of light, a reflection off a metallic object coming at you, and the training kicks in. In an instant you're fighting for your life, but you're confident you'll win.

In 2000, I was working in St. Paul as a security manager. As I was waiting for my third shift officers one evening, I was talking with my staff. I glanced at the camera monitors and noticed a guy walking down a service hall. He was pulling on door knobs as he walked by. He got to one door that was broken. The door was set up so that it would open about an inch, but there was a chain inside that wouldn't let it go any further. As I watched this guy on the camera, he started pulling on the door as hard as he could. When I saw him stick his foot up against the door jamb while he was pulling on the knob, I decided that was enough. I told my staff I was going to check it out.

I ran back to the service hall and found the guy smoking a cigarette in the loading dock. I told him he couldn't smoke in the building and asked what he was looking for. He told me he was looking for a bathroom. I told him I would show him where the restroom is. I am about six feet tall and average around 260 pounds; this guy was at least six feet five, and he had to be all of 250-260 pounds, solid. He had a considerable size advantage on me, and he was in a lot better shape than I was. I escorted him to a restroom and tried to signal one of the other officers to call the police, but they didn't see me on camera.

When he came out of the bathroom, he headed for the nearest door. It was locked. As I was saying, "Sorry, that door is locked," he realized the same thing, turned around, and headed for me. Before I could finish my sentence with, "What were you doing in the—?" he drew back and took a big roundhouse swing at me. I recognized it just in time to keep his fist from connecting square with my face, but he hooked my glasses. The glasses flew off my face, leaving a couple of small cuts on my cheek by my eye. I blocked a second punch and grabbed his shoulders; he grabbed mine. We stood there staring at each other for a second or two, locked shoulder to shoulder, unable to move each other.

I stepped back and pulled to try to get him off balance. This was in a hallway. In an instant, we started throwing each other back and forth from one side to another, slamming each other into the walls in the hallway. At one point, he spun me around and lifted me up high enough that I was a couple inches above a drinking fountain when I hit the wall. When the adrenaline starts pumping in a violent encounter, time seems to slow down. This fight went on for what seemed like four to five minutes, but we just so happened to have a camera in that hallway and when we viewed the tape, in was more like forty-five seconds.

After throwing each other around a little, I finally got my arm above his shoulder. I jumped up and threw all my weight into him. I was able to bring him down to the floor face down in what ended up being a modified arm bar—modified to the point that he was able to pull his way out of it. I ended up face down on the floor myself, the man standing over me. As I tried to turn over and ready myself for what might come next, I looked at a window a few feet from us and could see his reflection. He had pulled his arm back and seemed ready to kneel down on me to start punching me in the back while I was lying there.

Suddenly, one of the other officers came running out from behind the security station and tackled this guy from behind. Out of the corner of my eye, I saw him bear-hug this guy from behind and drop him on the ground. They wound up face down on the floor, the officer on top of this guy. He kept yelling, "OK! OK! I'll stop! I'm done!" Police showed up, reports were given, and everyone went their separate ways.

This particular event stood out in my mind from other incidents because the guy was a serious challenge for me. He was bigger, stronger, and he knew how to fight. Almost every time I make a citizen's arrest or take someone down, I get threats. Usually I hear things like "I am going to come back some night and take you out when you least expect it" or "I will come back and 'bleed' you"—that sort of thing. I have dealt with lots of death threats over the years. This time, though, the guy was making threats of harm while the cops were standing right there, and he wasn't even intoxicated. This made me a little more nervous than usual.

The human reaction to a threat of harm is a combination of energy and fear. Finding a balance between the two creates the ability to respond effectively. Some hit the lights and hammer on the gas every chance they get; some always volunteer to be the first one through the door. The hardest thing the adrenaline junkie has to deal with is making sure the energy doesn't completely drown out the fear.

Some look for employment in public safety almost as if looking for peace from a tragedy of their own. I met a guy a number of years ago who worked in security. He wanted to be a cop so he could make a difference, as his brother had overdosed on drugs when he was younger. It was almost as if he had entered law enforcement with a chip on his shoulder. He seemed to jump from job to job, having problems with excessive force at each one. There is a huge difference between someone who wants to be a cop to fight crime and someone who wants to be a cop to get revenge for something a criminal did.

The largest number of people I have met just feel compelled to protect and serve. Is there some great reward? No, not really. In fact, it is pretty much universally accepted throughout the public safety community that you will never get paid what you are really worth for the sacrifices you make. No one is ever going to get rich being a soldier, cop, or firefighter. So, again, why do they do it? The adrenaline junkies get their fix once in a while, and others get the chance to honor the memory of a loved one.

Many get the chance at some point in their career to do something truly heroic, the chance to feel like they have really made a difference in someone's life. A few may even get the chance at vindication, the opportunity to face overwhelming fear and overcome it. Ultimately, every professional risks everything to help others for the same reason each of us should. We all get injured once in a while. Every one of us may need someone to watch our back someday. Hollywood has created hundreds of films about one lone hero who takes out an entire army, the guy who single-handedly takes down the mob. However, the reality is that even the best special operations personnel need back up.

Think about it this way: A young man is working on a lower floor of the Twin Towers on 9-11-01. He sells insurance. Let's call him Tom. The plane hits the building, and he is one of many who run down several flights of stairs to get out of the building. As he is running out the door, he stops for a moment to watch as half a dozen firefighters run into the building. He stops running a couple blocks from the building. Out of breath, he sits down on the sidewalk, looks up, and sees the smoke and fire. As he talks with others who can't believe what they are seeing, the building collapses.

Fighting the shock of the moment, they stand up to run from the smoke, dust, and debris coming down the street. He feels fear and shock but also a sense of gratitude that he was able to get out of the building. Within a split second, this turns to an overwhelming, heart-wrenching pain as he remembers the firefighters he watched run into the building with no hesitation.

Tom goes on to have a normal life. He falls in love. They have a daughter. Life is good for Tom, but he never forgets the faces of the firefighters as they ran into the building. One of the firefighters Tom passed as he left the tower that day survived the collapse. We will call him Joe. Joe is injured that day but goes on to serve as a firefighter for many more years, never to forget his friends who didn't survive. He has a daughter as well.

Years later, Joe's daughter is grown up. She is walking down the street one day on her way to see a friend. Two guys walk up behind her, grab her by the arms, and head for a van on the street. She is kicking and screaming, but one guy has his hand over her mouth. They get within a few feet of the van when it just so happens that Tom walks out of the building they are in front of. He runs down a few stairs and jumps on one of the guys, forcing him to the ground. The other guy lets go of the girl and starts punching him.

Several cars roll by on the street as this is taking place. Finally one stops, and the driver starts dialing her phone. Another car stops. A guy jumps out and runs up to pull one of the thugs off Tom. The driver in the van is yelling, and the thugs realize what is going on. They both jump into the van, the driver guns the engine and they are gone in a flash. Tom has a couple of broken ribs and his face is pretty beat up. Other than that, he is fine. Joe's daughter is fine. She thanks him over and over. The police arrive and Joe's daughter tells them what happened; others tell police what they saw as well. One of the drivers who stopped gives the police the van's license plate number. It is later found abandoned.

Later on, Joe wants to thank the guy who jumped into harm's way to help his daughter. Tom and Joe meet. As Joe shakes Tom's hand, thanking him for saving his daughter, Tom remembers and recognizes his face. He grabs Joe's hand with both hands and thanks him. Joe is as dependent on Tom for his freedom and safety as Tom is on Joe.

This story is a fictitious example of countless similar stories I have heard of citizens who have jumped into a fight without hesitation. It seems everyone has a story about a hero. Sometimes it is someone they knew, but many times it is someone they didn't know and never saw again. Many of the stories I have heard were accounts from people who came into the emergency room. Sometimes it was the victim; other times, the hero; and once in a while, the person we were treating was the perpetrator. As doctor and nurses tend to the injured, we help the medical staff find out what happened from the bystanders, other victims, friends, and family.

The whole point of this story is the idea that public safety personnel are just as dependent on us as we are on them. Every firefighter out there hopes and prays every night that God will protect his family when he is working, just like we do. If his wife gets in a car accident on the way to work, he is hoping some good citizen will stop and help or at least call for help. Do we care about each other enough, do we love each other enough to make the same sacrifices to protect each other as we would to protect ourselves? If we do not, our freedoms will erode.

FREEDOM!

PEOPLE OFTEN FEAR WHAT THEY don't understand. We are afraid of people who aren't like us or don't agree with what we think is right. Over time, this fear can grow into hatred. Some men will hate others because of their skin color. Others will fear people from other nations because they don't understand what they are saying. Even in America, groups will always be separated by religious, political, and cultural differences. Every man and woman has the right to live life with his or her own religious and cultural beliefs. We create laws to insure everyone has the right to live life according to their beliefs, and we insure each has the right to voice those beliefs as well as discuss and debate them with others. This is the beauty of freedom.

Unfortunately, many people don't understand the core of these rights. The modern interpretation is that anyone can believe whatever they want as long as they keep it to themselves. You can't talk about what you believe, as you might offend someone. This is not free speech, and it creates fear, not freedom. In this environment, we allow fear to influence our judgment, and during that process we become unwilling to discuss or even listen to anything that does not follow what we believe, such as our view of what is right and wrong. Anyone who does not instantly agree with what we say thus becomes an "enemy." This has an impact on every aspect of society, from public safety to our economy. This has to change.

We don't teach civics in schools anymore. In light of this and many other factors, recent generations have lost sight of the most important aspect of our constitutional rights. The purpose of recognizing these rights in our nation's founding documents is to remind every citizen that everyone has the same rights. Your neighbor's rights are as important as your own. We are free in this country to do or say just about anything to our hearts' desire as long as our actions do not infringe on someone else's rights.

People from all over the world, rich and poor, risk everything to come to America. Some come here to escape oppression. In some countries, the oppression is inflicted on its citizens by the government itself. In other countries, the government is so unstable that individuals or groups of people run the country. Generally, these people are the ones with the most money and guns. Examples include Columbian drug lord Pablo Escobar, Mohammed Farrah Aidid in Somalia, Chechen rebels in Beslan, Al Qaeda in Afghanistan, Idi Amin in Uganda, Saddam Hussein in Iraq, Muammar al-Qaddafi in Libya, Fidel Castro in Cuba, and Kim Jong Il, now Kim Jong Un, of North Korea. The genocides in Rwanda and Bosnia were a result of this as well.

In most countries, people really don't know what it is like to have the simple freedom of making their own decisions. Instead, drug lords, mafia leaders, and terrorist groups tell them what they can do or can't do, what they can or can't believe. Anyone who opposes them is tortured and killed along with their families. This is not something unique to recent times; throughout recorded history, we see this is the way parts of the world have been run. Countries have risen and fallen. Wars have taken millions of lives as self-appointed leaders have attempted to gather up a group of people and take over a kingdom.

For example, the oppression in communist Russia became so destructive that Russian officials could not hide it anymore. President Ronald Reagan was able to convince Gorbachev that ending the Cold War would benefit the Russian economy as well as improve international relations. When the Berlin Wall was torn down, people from all over the world tried to help the citizens of Russia usher in a new age of freedom. In the years that followed, the economy in Russia collapsed. Many died of starvation. Why? There were plenty of farms. There were plenty of factories and industrial plants.

Russian factories made everything you can think of. For decades, they manufactured some of the most advanced aircraft, tanks, machinery, missiles, and spacecraft the world has ever seen. Did these people suddenly disappear? Were all of the factories and technology suddenly destroyed? Of course not.

The farms were there, the factories were there, the technology was there—so why was the country collapsing? Why were people starving? I remember countless stories in the news about grocery stores in Moscow with no bread. In America, we tend to take this for granted. We sit in front of the TV and wonder, "How can there be no bread at the store?" Russia's economic troubles after the fall of communism were the result of a complex set of problems, but we can use bread to explain the root cause.

There were farmers in Russia who had grain in their storage bins but no way to get it to a mill. The communist government told the farmer who he could sell the grain to, for how much, and when. In fact, the government bought the grain directly from the farmer, decided how much he was going to get paid for it, and shipped it to a mill.

There were also grain mills in Russia. Again, government officials decided how the grain was brought to the mill, how it would be processed, where the flour would be shipped, and how much the employees in the mill were going to get paid. The government even decided who was going to drive the truck from the farm to the mill and who was going to work in the mill. When the government collapsed, the established organizational structure collapsed with it.

We take our freedom for granted in America. Think of it this way:

Larry is an average guy living out in rural Minnesota. He knows a couple of farmers. One of the farmers is too busy to drive the corn, soybeans, or wheat to and from the mill, so he hires Larry part time to drive his truck for him. Another farmer approaches his boss and asks, "Would Larry be able to drive my grain to the mill as well? I can pay him for his time and pay you for using your truck to haul my grain." Pretty soon, Larry is driving full time. He can't even keep up with the demand for his time! Larry eventually realizes that he could start his own business instead of working for the farmer. He could buy his own truck, set his own price, and set his own hours.

He figures out how much he will need to charge to pay for a truck, insurance, and expenses. He goes to a bank to get a loan. He makes a decision, and in an instant, Larry is an entrepreneur. His business grows. He buys another truck and hires another driver. His customers like his work. He is honest, on time with deliveries, on time with bills, and on time with payments. Word spreads quickly, and now he has trucks driving all over the country delivering everything from corn to lumber to stereos. Larry is living the American dream.

This is freedom. This is free market economics, a simple process of seeing a need, having an idea to meet the need, and charging a fee to make it happen. This was lost in Russia. Decades of life in a society that punished independent thinking and freedom of expression destroyed the people's ability to even consider concepts of freedom that we so easily take for granted. A simple thought such as, "You know, someone should get a truck and ask this farmer for a fee to start hauling his grain for him," would have never occurred to Russian workers. The concept or ambition to do this without being told was destroyed by years of communist oppression. The average citizen had no concept of this freedom.

Free markets balance themselves. If Larry is the only guy in the county with a trucking service, he may start to get greedy. After he has a large customer base, he may decide to raise his prices. The local farmers now have no choice but to pay Larry's prices or their grain will spoil in the bins. Seems unfair, right? Well, freedom always creates a solution. Robert is one of Larry's drivers. Robert hears the farmers complaining about Larry raising his prices, so Robert decides to buy a truck and go into business for himself. Now Larry is forced to either lose customers or lower his prices. We could take this scenario on for hours. What if Robert gets greedy too? Someone else will naturally step in.

Robert has every constitutional right to pursue his dreams. Larry does too. Both of them have the right to provide a service and get paid for the service, and they both have the right to raise or lower prices to compete for customers. Customers will often choose whoever is cheapest, but the cheapest price won't always get the grain to market on time. The truck driver with the cheapest price may be using an unreliable truck. He may end up with only half his load getting to market, or none at all. Who pays the price for that? Eventually, the trucker and the farmer will pay a price for greed that leads to poor decisions.

The only responsibility the government has is to make sure that Robert doesn't do anything that takes away Larry's constitutional rights and vice versa. Neither of them can do anything that might harm or take away the life of the other. They both have the freedom to start a business, provide a service, charge a price for the service, compete for customers, buy equipment, sell equipment, and make a profit.

The government should not tell either of them how much they can charge. The government should not tell either of them what type of truck to buy. The responsibility of the government is to make sure the roads are in good condition. The government must provide a well-equipped public safety force, including enforcing laws that require Tom and Joe to keep their trucks in safe working condition. Other than that, the government's responsibility is to get out of the way so both men can live the American dream.

We have observed something similar in Iraq and Afghanistan. We hear a lot about American "contractors" working in Iraq. Usually, the only contractors we hear about are the paramilitary security services in armored Suburbans. The ones we don't hear about are all the "contractors" all over the country teaching the Iraqi people how to build power plants and water treatment facilities. Business men from all over the world are teaching the people of Iraq how to start a business, build schools, and harness the country's natural resources.

I was watching the news a few years ago when a story came on about the economy in Iraq after Saddam Hussein was captured. The story centered on car sales; people in Iraq were buying cars as fast as the dealerships could get them. Car dealerships were opening all over the country. The most challenging thing for most of the citizens was the freedom to choose which color of car they would like! Several Iraqi car dealers were interviewed. They said there were plenty of vehicles, new and used, as well as plenty of customers ready to buy; the Iraqi people were simply struggling with how to handle the freedom to choose what color, make, and model of car to buy, not to mention interior colors, stereo options, and other accessories. If was almost as if they were scared to make a decision for themselves.

In America, we have our own groups who try to use power, money, guns, and terror to try to influence people. Street gangs started out small but quickly gained popularity and influence. What started out as a way for inner-city kids to try to protect each other grew into turf wars over who was allowed in what neighborhoods. This then developed into who could sell drugs in what neighborhoods, and these powerful groups were quickly taken over by greedy, ruthless leaders. This has nothing to do with protecting each other anymore. All that matters is money and power, any way they can get it.

What once was an almost noble ideal turned into petty grudges about who was allowed to walk which streets. Power struggles grew into bloody wars, innocent children gunned down as cowards opened fire on their rivals. Now these gangs have been overshadowed by even more powerful international groups. MS-13 has crept into American society in ways that Al Capone could only dream of. How is this possible? Simply put, it is easier to give your life away to someone who says they will take care of you than it is to provide for yourself. There is comfort in this if you were raised to believe there is nothing you can do about it anyway. If you were raised to believe you have the freedom to do anything you want as long as you are willing to work hard to get it, this is voluntary slavery.

In many ways, our freedoms allow for this. We recognize that everyone has the same constitutional rights as us. "Innocent until proven guilty" will create, in some, the desire to take what others have. The reward is worth the risk of the consequences. Law enforcement keeps trying to build a better mouse trap, and criminals keep coming up with ways to defeat the trap. Again, freedom allows for both. Until the mouse (a citizen) steals someone's cheese, he has not committed a crime. He has the same rights and freedoms as any other citizen. Likewise, if a police officer looks the other way while a drug deal is taking place, he isn't a crime fighter anymore.

In many parts of the world, the average person works much harder than the average American. Over the years I have had the opportunity to work with people from all over the world. Some have worked for me, some were professional acquaintances, and others were just people I became friends with. Many were the hardest-working people I have ever met. They were truly grateful for whatever they had, however little that may be. A number of years ago, a man from Liberia worked for me. We were talking once about America and freedom when he told me, "People in my country really believe that money grows on trees in America." They imagine that there is so much opportunity, wealth, and freedom here that all you have to do is show up, walk down the street, and pick it off the trees.

America is the land of opportunity. Anyone can find a job here. Any citizen, or anyone with a green card, can walk into any company and fill out an application. Even if you are here illegally, you still have a fairly good chance at finding work. For the amount of work required, people in America get paid more than almost anywhere in the world. Everyone with the basic qualifications for a job has an equal chance of getting the job. It is not the government's responsibility to find you a job; you need to go out and ask for a job so you can make a living.

Anyone can get an education in America as well. It will cost you, but you don't have to attend an Ivy League school for it to be worthwhile. Almost anyone can afford a technical college degree. If you don't have the money, there are loans and private funds that anyone can tap into. But again, you are the one who needs to go out and study hard to get an education to get the job you want and pursue your dreams. America has no shortage of anything. There are grocery stores everywhere, and if you are poor, there are food banks, soup kitchens, and organizations like the Salvation Army that help millions every year.

Are we the only country with jobs? No! Are we the only country where someone can get an education? No! Are we the only country who helps the poor and homeless? No! So, why do people want to come to America more than any other country? We often hear people say that the rest of the world really doesn't like Americans at times because we are arrogant. Many Americans do seem to act like we are better than everyone else—this is very true. But anywhere you go in the world, you will find that the same people who may not like Americans for some reason do respect Americans.

They see Americans voluntarily join the military to spend part of their lives protecting and serving people in some country on the other side of the world. They see American missionaries and private organizations volunteering to help people in every corner of the globe. America isn't the only country that does this, but we lead the rest of the world in doing so. America isn't just the land of equal job opportunity; it is the land of equal opportunity to speak your mind and be heard. This is the land of equal respect, the land of equal opportunity to make a difference in this world. Government doesn't create this respect; this equal respect created our government.

Again, this is not something new or unique to America. Our principles of rights and freedoms were recognized throughout the history of the world. The Roman Empire changed from a dictatorship to a republic more than once. The Magna Carta was one of the first documents in history to establish a form of government that recognized the rights of the people no matter who was ruling the land. This guided our Founding Fathers. America is by no means perfect, but our Constitution permanently established the ideals of freedom that men have sought for centuries.

Throughout history, men have fought for freedom and sought to establish governments that would recognize their rights. Unfortunately, the most powerful ruler with the largest army usually became king. Millions of people have died as a result of war, kings, rulers, dictators and warlords picking fights with each other. Why does God allow this pain and suffering? Why did He allow Adolf Hitler to become as powerful as He did? Why didn't He just inflict him with some disease rather than require so many people to die to defeat him? God could wipe out any enemy with one breath.

War in ancient times involved one group of soldiers running into another group of soldiers with swords, blood flying everywhere. Battle in those days was gruesome. Swords, spears, axes, knives, clubs, and arrows were the weapons used. Men were split open and left to bleed to death on the battlefield. The only way to survive was to injure the enemy just enough to insure that the opponent could not fight anymore. Thus, it often took hours for the injured to finally die on the battlefield. Soldiers often call out to God as all hell is breaking loose around them but walk away from combat doubting whether God is real. The same question is asked over and over again: How can an all-powerful, loving God allow men to do this to each other?

Some religions teach their followers that God wants to wipe out people who do not believe in Him or oppose His plan, suggesting that God wants us to do His dirty work for Him. If He cares enough to die for all men, He is not going to hurt those He loves. We each have an equal chance with God. He does not play favorites with men; no matter how bad we are, God wants to give every man every possible chance to repent and receive forgiveness. God gave us the ability to make our own choices, whether good or bad. Of course God wants us to choose to do right. He wants every person to have the longest and happiest possible life. Our inherent God-given freedom allows us the opportunity to choose to do wrong, but that same freedom allows the opportunity for forgiveness and change.

We can't control another person's decision to do wrong, but we have the right to protect ourselves from harm that may be caused by other people's choices. No matter the circumstance, God will protect those who call out to Him for help. It can be difficult for people to grasp these concepts, yet the most important principle can often be the most difficult to grasp. Our inherent rights and freedoms require us to see other people the way God sees them. This is the essence of freedom.

Freedom is not something we get—it is something we give to each other. The only reason we have it is because we give it to each other and believe it will be given back in return. The government doesn't create it; it merely recognizes it by creating rules that punish those who take freedom away from another. The church doesn't create it, either; it only explains how God intended for us to use it. Freedom was born into every human being long before any church or government was ever conceived.

Every soldier in our military is trained to fight, but most are support personnel. Someone needs to drive the trucks that deliver supplies to the men fighting on the front lines. Someone needs to order those supplies. Someone needs to be in the band to entertain the troops and celebrate the victories. The generals plan the attacks, while the frontline troops carry out the orders. The Air Force needs more pilots for reconnaissance and airlifts than it does for fighter aircraft. Every soldier may face combat someday, yet every soldier must also be able to do more than fight and kill.

The same principle holds true for us as well. A select few of us are police, but every citizen has the authority to arrest another for a crime. Do you know how to use this authority? A select few of us are firemen. Even if you aren't one, would you be willing to run into your neighbor's burning house with a fire extinguisher to save one of his kids? Would you hope he would do the same for one of your kids? Everyone should know how to perform CPR, even if you don't work in healthcare.

The history of the world could basically be described as an endless series of nations attacking each other in an attempt to become more and more powerful. This drive to conquer seems to be a basic aspect of human nature and follows the general principle that law enforcement and security professionals live by. If you have something of value, someone will try to take it from you if you give them the opportunity, no matter how big or small the item is. This includes our freedom. I do not believe that all people are crooks. In fact, the vast majority of people inhabiting our planet are honest, hard-working citizens, but there will always be a small percentage of people who give in to temptation. There will always be an even smaller percentage who just don't care about anyone other than themselves.

Each of us has a right to voice our beliefs without being afraid of harm. We have a responsibility to discuss our beliefs with others in a respectful manner, whether others agree with us or not. This requires each of us to be willing to listen to other opinions and beliefs without being offended. You don't have to agree; you just need to be willing to listen. I am not going to suggest that you can't get upset. By all means, if you are passionate about what you believe, then show it. But you must remember that the other guy has the "right" to get angry as well. You also need to bear in mind that many people will stop listening to you if you get angry. That is their right as well! This healthy exchange of ideas creates thought, building academia and industry. This is how we grow—by listening to, and learning from, each other. This separates us from the animals. Too many have died to give us this right in the first place; we cannot squander it by being selfish and petty.

Each individual is responsible for making their own life the best it can be. The Declaration of Independence does not describe a right to happiness—it describes a right to pursue happiness. We have the right to go out and find it. It also says no one can take away your rights unless you let them. Likewise, no one is responsible for making you happy. You have the ability to learn, build, create, and achieve. When you do this, you can offer something that other people want, and this allows you to profit from your hard work and enjoy life. It is your responsibility to work hard and make good decisions so you can find your happiness.

The only purpose of the government is to make sure no one gets in your way. In doing so, the government makes sure you don't get in anyone else's way either. If you do something that takes away someone else's God-given rights, you lose yours. The government cannot protect you from yourself, your own stupidity and greed. The only way for the government to do this is to take away your freedom, and even then, it never works.

Soldiers, police, and firefighters will never replace the responsibility each of us has to protect each other. The only way we can make sure no one interferes with our freedom is to make sure each of us does whatever we can to help protect each other's freedoms. We love our families. We love our kids. We love our friends. In order to make sure the next generation can enjoy the God-given rights we have now, each of us must decide to serve and protect each other now—not just for our loved ones, but for all of our neighbors.

This is why we give money to churches, food bank and other organizations that help people in need. Many of us volunteer to serve meals at a homeless shelter or give blood to help save lives. We don't give because a law or government official tells us to; we give simply because we choose to. The government should not be in the business of charity. When the government takes our tax money from our pockets and gives it to someone else in need, they take a cut and pocket the money for doing so. We should have the freedom to choose what we believe is important. We exercise this freedom by choosing where our money goes. You should even have the freedom to choose not to give to charity at all. Just remember, you reap what you sow.

We each have a responsibility to stand up for what is right. To this end, the most important thing you can do is vote. Don't let anyone tell you your vote does not count—it does! The average hard-working American barely has time to make dinner, pay the bills, and spend time with the kids. Most don't have time to write their congressman or go to political rallies, but you can certainly vote. Even more importantly, you must be willing to talk with your family, friends, and neighbors about important issues in a civil manner. Listen and discuss. Respect other opinions, even when you don't agree.

You will probably never find a politician that agrees with everything you believe, but you can find the one you agree with the most. Politicians generally fall into one of two categories: those who don't trust the people to make their own decisions, and those who do. If you are hiring someone to make decisions about your life, do you think it is better to hire someone who is afraid of you, or someone who listens to you? Don't vote because of emotion—vote with your conscience. This is the only way to insure no one takes away the constitutional rights and freedoms that so many have died for. Your vote may be the only voice you have, but it has a lot of power behind it.

ADAM & EVE, MEN & WOMEN

MEN AND WOMEN ARE DIFFERENT from each other in a wide variety of ways, both mentally and physically. Men's bodies function differently than women's do. The hormone and chemical composition of a woman's body is different than a man's, and this includes the brain. As such, men respond differently to emotional stimulus, stress, and adrenaline than women, leading to distinct differences in emotional reactions and cognitive responses. The feminist movement has spent the last several decades attempting to push society to view men and women as the same. As more and more research studies attempt to support this notion, they find more proof that men and women are very different. Some people seem to believe this is somehow a bad thing, but simply put, it isn't.

Just to clarify a point, men and women are different but equally valuable. Whether you believe this is God's design or natural selection really does not matter; it is true. Men and women both have inherent strengths that help to balance out each other's weaknesses. The result is that men and women are equally valuable and important, specifically to each other. Allow me to explain.

The term "marriage" means to make two separate things into one single thing. Not a temporary attachment, but a permanent unity that, once complete, no one can tell that the item was once two separate things. God created men to be, in many ways, uncontrollable. Men are designed to seek adventure. God designed women to provide a way to maintain some control over men, a way to calm them down and keep them focused. Women can hold a great deal of control over the men in their lives (husbands, sons, fathers, brothers) by using what God has given them: love, honor, passion, and respect. Having said this, men and woman must understand the way God intended for this to work.

Men are, by nature, resistant to being controlled. We resist someone telling us what to do, and we make every effort to be the masters of our own environment. The need to seek adventure is in all men, whether they are in love with a woman or have a family or not. Men often look at life with the attitude "Wherever I am is home." The cowboys of the Old West were perfectly content to sleep out under the stars, but all people inherently desire companionship.

Women are focused on making things clean and balanced, bringing everything the family needs into one comfortable place and creating a stable home environment. This becomes the place the family gathers together for safety, the place where children are brought up. Every man desires the stability, safety, comfort, and companionship of home, but each will leave to seek adventure again.

These differences create balance. A couple's respective strengths create a desire and need for the other. The result is that a man and a woman become dependent on each other, allowing them to meet each other's needs. This principle applies even before a man is married or in love. A teenage boy wants to leave home to seek excitement. He wants to get a job, go to college, and be independent—and yet he will always be pulled home again by the allure of clean laundry, a hot meal, and other comforts of home.

The more a woman tries to remove or stifle a man's inherent desire for freedom, the more he will resist. When we refer to a man going out to seek adventure, this is not necessarily referring to a long trip to conquer another country. It could be a hunting trip for a couple of days. It could be a job interview. For most men, this adventure is the basic daily trek to work and the return home each day.

Most men are not raised to understand the dynamics of relationships. As a result, men often attempt to blame the women in their lives for "holding them back" or "stifling their needs as men." The reality is that men need to understand relationships so they can properly manage their own behaviors. Men need to act like men! Honest, loving, passionate, strong men. In doing so, men need to resist temptation and learn to talk earnestly with the women in their lives. Each man needs to learn how to serve the needs of the people he loves and provide leadership in his family. If you aren't clear on this, keep reading.

Any person, man or woman, will base their opinion of themselves on what others think. The knowledge of good and evil creates in us a self-centered view of the world. We become focused on "me." As a child, our innocence keeps us pure; at this point our emotions are pure, but we are still learning how to give and receive love. From the very beginning of our lives we desire love, the attention and affection of others.

Love, in this most innocent and pure condition, is, by nature, selfish. Basically, *I* want to be loved, and *I* want to give love the way *I* want so *I* feel good. However, this mindset creates a desire to act to receive love from others. This is the way God views us as well. If we are nurtured, this love will mature. The result is unconditional love directed more toward others than ourselves, even if they don't love us back. That is why the Bible states that God is a "jealous" God. There are several references to this, including Exodus 20:5 and 2 Corinthians 11:2. His love for us creates in Him a desire for us to love Him back. That is why He sent His Son to Earth, and that is why Jesus was willing to be sent.

We are taught to love by the people we care about the most—our parents, grandparents, brothers, sisters, and friends. The ability to love others is very dependent on the ability to love ourselves, and the ability to love *me* is based on my opinion of myself. My opinion of myself is based on the love I receive, or don't receive, from the people I care about the most. Encouragement, praise, and kind words like "Good job!", "I love you," "You are so smart!", "You look absolutely beautiful," "You are such a handsome young man," "I couldn't have asked for a better son/daughter," "I am so proud of you," and so on make all the difference. These statements and loving, supportive actions will mold the view children have of themselves.

The opposite will do the same. Constant criticism will make children critical of themselves. This creates fear—fear of doing the wrong thing and fear of failure. Children eventually stop trying and just stop caring about anything, because they can't find any reason to care about themselves. Positive or negative, this perspective is carried into adulthood. As adults, we lose some of the objectivity, the benefit of the doubt that we had as children. We make assumptions as to what we *think* others like or dislike about us. If we receive love and respect as a child, we tend to have healthy relationships as an adult.

When a man does not receive admiration, love, affection, enjoyment, and, yes, sex from the woman he loves, he starts looking for fulfillment from something else outside the home, like work. He will eventually look for it in another woman. Women don't often realize this. When a man really believes the woman he loves enjoys being physically close and intimate with him, it creates the type of self-confidence and passion for life that gives a man the belief that he can take on any challenge, the feeling that he can win any battle, the confidence that he can conquer the world.

Women have a great deal of influence over the men who love them. A supportive mother giving sincere love, admiration, and affection can have a great deal of control in her son's ultimate destiny by encouraging him to strive for greatness. A controlling mother withholding this will have the opposite effect. A wife has something more: the ability to give or take away pleasure and intimacy. Men were designed to resist control and be independent. Men and women who cheat on their spouse are often looking for the admiration, attention, and time spent with the opposite sex that can either make or break our sense of self-confidence and self-worth. However, that is not an acceptable excuse. Cheating is still wrong.

Often times, sincere love is something a man never had while he was growing up. This creates an emptiness that sex alone can't fill, so he keeps looking for it the rest of his life. Most men have not been raised with the ability to understand love beyond sex. Despite this, that does not mean they don't still long for it or need it! No matter how much sex the man has with his wife or other women, he will never find the "love" he is really looking for because he wasn't raised to understand the difference. Of course, many women are raised without this understanding as well, and they will spend their lives doing the same thing.

I hug my kids all the time and tell them I love them, my daughter and my sons. Most men don't do this because they were raised without this affection, but I want my kids to grow up understanding the difference between a hug from a good friend or relative and a hug from a spouse or potential spouse. Sons need regular hugs from their moms just as daughters need regular hugs from their dads. Children who do not experience regular affection as they grow up have trouble understanding the difference between love and lust, and this is one of the primary reasons some relationships die right from the beginning. This is also part of the reason our society has so many single moms. Relationships are not based on love and commitment; they are based on emotion and pleasure.

Emotions change and fade, but love grows. If the only time a person experiences the emotion and pleasure of hugging another person is during sex, it will never mean anything more to them. Men and woman both want to be desired and held but often have trouble being affectionate without sex. Women have different needs for sexual pleasure than men do. Men need to learn to enjoy the balance, the ability to give intimacy and pleasure as well as receive it.

There is a difference between making love and having sex. The first time you ride a new roller coaster is pure adrenaline. Some of the excitement wears off after the tenth ride, but the ride is still fun. You may hold on tight the first couple of times and then try raising your hands to change the experience. If you spend your life being upset that the tenth roller coaster ride isn't as exciting as the first, you won't have anything to look forward to until the next roller coaster is built. You will just be sitting on a park bench when you could still be enjoying the ride like everyone else! If all you care about is sex, you will get bored fast. With the right mindset, making love together is always fun and exciting even years later. This has less to do with the physical act and more to do with the person you do it with. It is, as with many things in life, what you make it to be.

Men naturally enjoy spending time with other men; women naturally enjoy being with other women. Men understand men better than women do, and vice versa. There is a natural love men have for each other, and a natural love women have for each other. Just as there is love between a brother and a sister, this love is not a sexual attraction or desire. Men who can't hug their sons will raise boys with a distorted understanding of this. These men at times turn to other men for love and intimacy, as it feels like he has found somebody who listens and enjoys spending time with him, someone who actually seems to really care.

This is based on true God-given love but is then distorted into sexual desire when the man has no experience with true love as God intended it. God's desire for us to love others is destroyed by unhealthy relationships that flourish because our ability to love is based on our opinion of ourselves. We base our opinion of ourselves on other people's perceptions rather than God's opinion of us, prioritizing what we think others like or dislike about us. As children, we have an innocent, Godly understanding of love that is either reinforced or distorted by our childhood relationships. This is the way we were created. Adam fell into temptation because his love for his wife was more important than his love for God. His opinion of himself became based more on Eve's opinion rather than God's.

We don't give the women in our lives the credit they deserve. Even into the 1800s, American frontier women and children worked just as hard as or harder than the men did to survive the trials of life. In most families, this still holds true today. The Bible tells us to love our wives as Christ loved the church. Think about that statement for a moment.

Imagine if you were to heat two pieces of metal to glowing, place them together, and pound them against each other with all your force. You continue the process of heating and reheating, pounding again and again. You would eventually turn the two separate pieces of metal into one single piece. When done correctly, no one will ever be able to tell that the piece was ever two separate pieces. BUT, in order for this to take place, for it to be done correctly, both pieces of steel must undergo change. Both must be melted, beaten, thrust into the fire, and then put into water to allow the very structure of both to blend and flow into the other.

This is not simply gluing two pieces of steel together. This is not bending a hook at the end of each and then just pounding the hooks together. As long as a seam can be seen with the eye, two items can be separated. A marriage is a connection of two items with no seam. Both pieces of steel change from what they were into something completely new. Even if the new single piece of steel is cut or broken into two separate pieces again, neither piece will transform back into what they were before they were married to the other. Part of either will always remain with the other. This process takes two people working together, one holding the pieces of metal while the other strikes with the hammer. They are not striking each other with the hammer; they are working together to create something. Creating this bond in a haphazard way will ultimately weaken and harm both people. If someone attempts to unite two pieces of metal but does not heat the metal enough to weaken it, the resulting bond will not be complete.

Likewise, if either person gives up before the bond is truly complete, the items will not be held in place correctly, or the one left doing the work will tire and become weak before the process is complete. Ultimately, the two pieces of metal will not be truly and completely bonded together, and both pieces will actually be made weaker. Both will eventually be broken. Neither will ever return to their original state. Both will remain broken until someone picks up the pieces and begins to heat and pound them into something new. In order for a marriage bond to be created, the work never truly stops; it is a lifetime of hard even dangerous work. A true marriage requires both people to completely trust the other. Both must become completely dependent on and vulnerable to the other, and both must be willing to completely submit to the other without hesitation. Anytime you place your total trust and dependence on another person, there is a very real risk of harm.

This work never ends, but it should become easier as the two people learn to work together and communicate with each other. Two people who care about each other will never want the other to be harmed physically or emotionally in any way. Together, they will still be required to face harm from others and each other, but they must always communicate and work together to learn what causes harm and how they both can prevent it. When the marriage commitment is made, both husband and wife choose to sacrifice themselves emotionally and physically for the other.

If two friends decide to go into business together, there is a partnership that is created. Let's say it's a construction company. One may be the best carpenter ever, and the other may be the best businessman ever. Each has his specialty. On the other hand, the builder may know very little about managing a business, while the businessman may know very little about how to frame a house. They rely on each other to make good decisions related to their respective experience. Each is responsible for a unique part of keeping the business running smoothly; neither is greater than the other. Both must work as hard as they can to keep their part of the business going.

They must also make sure they work together and consult with each other on all aspects and decisions related to the business, regardless of whether one is the expert in that particular area or not. The builder can't just go out and purchase a new piece of equipment without seeking approval from his partner. There may be a legitimate argument that the business absolutely needs that piece of equipment, but this decision must be made together; regardless of the reason,. The business expert cannot go out and hire an accountant without seeking the approval of his partner. The business expert knows it is needed. He will know what to expect from the accounting firm, but the builder will not. Thus, the businessman will probably be the one to decide which accountant to hire, but he can't do so without first seeking the approval of his partner.

Marriage is the same way. Any relationship must run much the same way, but this is especially true in regard to marriage. There will be one who ultimately has the final word on any given issue, the one with the greatest authority in regard to that particular arena, but that person must also respect their partner. They must listen and learn from their partner and never operate without full disclosure. Partners understand that they are equal.

One of the greatest men I have ever worked for explained his management philosophy to me this way. In order for me to be an effective employer or manager of other people, I need to treat my employees as my customers. They work for me. I am in charge, but they are the ones doing the work. I can't have a business without employees. If my staff are appreciated and satisfied with my work, they will be more productive. If they know I am committed to doing my best for them, they will be more committed to doing their best for me.

Almost all of us understand the principles of customer satisfaction. Whether you are an owner or an employee, all of us are customers at times. All of us can recognize the difference between good customer service and bad customer service. So, this is my challenge for you: Is your ultimate goal to provide the best customer service you can for your wife, your husband, your kids, and your family? If not, don't be surprised when they start shopping someplace else.

GOD'S LOVE

LET'S TAKE THE METALWORK EXAMPLE one step further. Iron, copper, gold, and other basic metal elements are mined out of the earth. A foundry takes the ores of various types of minerals and mixes them together to create a particular type of metal, be it steel, bronze, stainless steel, and so on. Is this metal created by just mixing the various ores together? No. The ores must be mixed together and then heated and melted at several thousand degrees to completely destroy everything the ores originally were and create something completely new. This molten metal is then poured out, glowing hot, into devices that form it into various shapes. God took various elements He had created in the Earth and pressed, heated, and shaped them Himself, creating all life on Earth.

As an example, let's look at a piece of round stock. Size really doesn't matter. The simplest device I can think of is a tent stake. To create one, a round metal rod is cut into sections about ten inches long. One end is cut slightly at an angle to create a crude point. The other end is a flat cut, but the last inch is bent over at ninety degrees. You drive the stake into the ground at an angle so that the bent end holds the corner of a tent to the ground. With little effort, almost anyone could make something similar in their garage. Yet, once this round, perfectly straight metal rod is changed into this simple device, it is changed forever and will never return to its original perfectly round, perfectly straight state.

If you try to straighten the stake, you will only ever come close. You can pound on it with a hammer to try to take the bend out, but no matter how much you pound, the point of the bend may look straight to the naked eye, but it will always be a little thinner and weaker than the rest of the rod. Even if you heat the rod and pound out the bend, you may get close to straight, but the pounding and heating will make that section thinner and leave small flat hammer marks all over the piece. It will never be as perfectly round or perfectly straight as it originally was when it came out of the press at the foundry, and thus it will never be as perfectly strong as it originally was when it was created. This principle applies to any metal object.

Think of a piece of steel used as a hoist point on a ship. A metal plate two, three, or even four inches thick is placed in a press under hundreds of tons of pressure to form it. Even if you place the same piece back into an even larger, more powerful press, you will never be able to bend the piece back perfectly straight. It will never return to its original state; it will forever be changed. To create nearly anything from metal, you must shape pieces of steel by heating and pounding them. You have to weaken the metal before you can make it stronger. So, what is my point?

We are created by God in our original state as perfectly straight, perfectly strong metal stock. However, God's intent for us is to become something useful to him and to others. He has a plan for each of us that we will be changed and molded into what He desires us to be. He uses life and the experiences we go through in life to alter us or change us into what He wants.

We may become part of a machine or structure at one point in our lives, then be removed and altered to become part of something else at a later point. Every experience we have from minute to minute in our lives, good or bad, thrusts us into the coals. Every comment a person makes about our work or appearance is another blow of the hammer. Every decision we make bends us ever so slightly into what we will become. As we are being struck by the hammer or placed in the press, our attitude and the choices we make become the most important part of this process.

At times, no matter how hard you try, a certain piece of metal just seems like it doesn't want to cooperate. You must toss it into the scrap pile and start over with a new piece of metal. There are times when we resist the heating, pounding, or bending God is trying to complete in our lives. We resist by having an attitude of anger or frustration with the changes in our lives. God is trying to take us in a new direction, but we just want to stay as we are. It may be fear of the unknown that prevents us from changing, or it may be that we are just comfortable with life as it is and become lazy. In this state, we resist change instead of thanking God for new opportunities. We make decisions out of fear rather than having faith. No matter how painful the changes may be, we must still have faith.

We all go through negative experiences in life—uncomfortable, challenging, painful experiences. Someone makes a comment about your work not being good enough or fast enough; you are thrust into the glowing coals. Someone close to you dies; the hammer swings and strikes you. These can, however, be positive experiences as well. You get a new job, and the hammer strikes you again. You have a son or daughter; you are bent in the press brake. Someone makes a comment about how nice your haircut looks, and you are thrust into the water to cool.

Every moment in life, good or bad, will alter you in some way. You are responsible for how each moment impacts you based on the choices you make and the attitude you have. If we resist what God is trying to do in our lives, He will not be able to mold us into what He ultimately needs us to be. He doesn't throw us away, though, even when we resist what He is trying to do for us. We might pull ourselves out of His hands and end up on the scrap pile for a period of time, but this is the best part: God never gets rid of anything in the scrap pile. He will never forget anything He has made. He remembers every one of us and makes an effort to use all of us in some way.

The more we resist, the less chance He will be able to find a use for us, the longer we will sit on the scrap pile, and the rustier we will get. We resist Him by trying to make ourselves into what we want to be rather than what He wants us to be. We never really know what His ultimate plan for us is, so how we can be most useful? You may be determined to become a gear on a bicycle when God's ultimate plan for you is to become a piston in a Harley. We resist because of fear. Fear is the lack of faith. The more we have faith in Him, the more He will be able to use us and mold us. He has the perfect plan for each person—the plan that He knows will make us the happiest person.

His perfect plan doesn't necessarily mean we will be molded into one thing and stay that way for the rest of our lives. Almost assuredly, we will go through many changes in life. We are attached to other people when we get married, have children, get a new job, join a church, join a club, and make friends. If you have faith in God and faith in other people, these connections become strong bonds that will last through time. If you resist, the connections will be weak, and He won't be able to use you to make a larger and more complex machine. You won't achieve the greatness He intends for you.

There will be times when you are cut from the machine. This may be a result of a bad choice you made in life, but it may also be God's plan to use you to start another even greater project. Someone you are close to may be cut away. This may be the result of a death or divorce or it may be the result of a simple thing like holding a grudge. You will feel hurt and loss. A part of you may be cut away with that person, and a part of that person may be left with you. You may be left damaged or rough around the edges. You may be permanently altered or scarred in some way. The only way for you to get past this is to allow God to grind away the damaged areas. This is painful, and it requires you to have faith that He knows what is best for you. The end result is a smooth, polished, and beautifully restored finish.

God is always there guiding our lives. He never leaves us. He never forgets about us. We all make choices in life, and we may at times choose to resist Him. All of us at one point or another end up on the scrap pile wishing we could relive a part of our lives. We all look back and wish we could change some of the decisions we have made. Don't waste your life regretting your past and the decisions you made. Instead, look up to God and pray for another opportunity to be molded into something new, the next chance to be used for a greater purpose.

This is the truth that every person needs to understand. No matter how rusty you are or how bent, damaged, and beaten you may be, no matter how jagged, broken, or cut up you are on the inside, no matter how much you have been hurt by other people or how bad you have been, and no matter how useless, ugly, or damaged you feel . . . God can pick you up off the scrap pile and place you back into the melting pot you originally came from before you were even born.

Only He can completely reform you into a brand-new piece of steel, perfectly strong, perfectly straight, and perfectly pure. He does this when we look up to him and pray, "Please forgive me. Please take away my pain and make me into whatever you want. I will do whatever you ask of me for the rest of my life, and I will be thankful for whatever I have every day."

The decision to let go of the past and have faith in God is not an easy one. It is often painful to be completely reformed and changed into something new, but the end result is freedom. We become new, and God can change you into something more beautiful than you ever thought possible.

We were created to serve him as we serve each other, but God's true desire for Adam was to have someone with whom he could develop a relationship, a friendship. He is still the one who created the world and everything in it, after all; we are not His equals. He has power and authority beyond anything we will ever understand, but He tells us that He will give us His power and authority if we truly believe in Him. Our trouble is that most of us won't ever allow ourselves to submit and truly embrace faith to that point.

We are created with the freedom to choose to love or not. When we love someone but that person does not love us back, this is the ultimate pain in life. Conversely, when we love someone and that person does love us back, this is the ultimate happiness in life. God loves us this way and created us with the freedom to choose to love Him back. The same desire to pour out love was given to Adam. He had a desire to love God but also love others.

God brought the animals to Adam and gave him the authority to name all of them. Living in farm country and having our own little hobby farm taught us a very important principle: If you have animals you plan to sell or raise to butcher, don't give them names! As soon as you give an animal a name, you have expressed love for that animal. We have the desire to take in pets because our capacity to love goes far beyond just people.

In order to maintain an understanding of the authority God has over us, He created the one single act of obedience. Adam and Eve could do anything they wanted on Earth. God had created the ultimate life of happiness for them. There was only one single thing they couldn't do: Out of the entire garden, out of the entire Earth, there was only *one single tree* they couldn't eat from. Pretty simple, pretty easy, right? Well, you would think so.

Adam and Eve had broken the one simple directive God had given them. A pure heart would admit to a wrongdoing and seek forgiveness. Eve now felt something new: guilt, the result of making the choice to do something you know you should not do. So, how do you know what you should not do? You may inherently know that you would not want someone else to do that to you, or some type of higher authority has told you "Don't do that." Generally, religious authorities explain that Eve was "disobedient" to God. This is true and important to recognize, but the term "disobedient" is much too simplistic. Settle back in your chair. Get comfortable, take a deep breath and exhale slowly because this will blow your mind.

God has given each of us the freedom and responsibility to disobey when we are told to do something that is unquestionably wrong. This is the core principle of freedom outlined in the Declaration of Independence, Constitution, and Bill of Rights. We are born with inherent rights that are given to us by God. Earthly authorities do not give us these rights. Earthly authorities, men, choose to recognize them as such or discount them. In fact, God created us with a free will giving us the capacity to disobey Him as well. Yes, you read that correctly. God created us with the ability to disobey him, but there is a problem with choosing to do so. Choosing to obey or disobey requires a person to make a judgment as to what is right and what is wrong.

How do you know what is right and what is wrong? At some point in your life you must develop some sort of inherent reference or standard in order to judge what is right and what is wrong in any given situation. Again, this may come from a base understanding that you would not want someone else to do such a thing to you. Or, it comes from a set of core believes, a code of conduct or values, that were instilled in you by some authority in your life, be it a Heavenly or an Earthly authority. If you follow the law, you are protected by the law. Driving is actually one of the most dangerous activities that we do. There is a chance that you may get into an accident even if you obey the speed limits, no passing zones and stay in your lane while driving. If you do get in an accident, public safety and the courts work to determine who is responsible for the damage. In this situation you have the ability to argue that the damage is not your fault because you were following the law. If you drive too fast or swerve into the other lane because you were not paying attention, you violated the law. The damage is your fault.

Our Founding Fathers made a determination that the laws imposed on them by the British were clear violations of their inherent, God given rights. The American Revolution was the result. I am grateful for their decision. Our laws are based on recognizing these inherent rights. As citizens, we often fail to recognize that obeying the laws that are created in such a nation will create the greatest level of safety and peace that mankind can achieve. However, these laws are still made by men. "Power tends to corrupt, and absolute power corrupts absolutely. Great men are almost always bad men." This phrase can be found in many forms throughout the history of written text, but is most often attributed to John - Dalberg Acton, Lord Acton (1834–1902) as an opinion expressed in a letter to Bishop Creighton in 1887. What does this phrase suggest? Given the opportunity, some will attempt to use their authority to create laws that violate our rights. So, how do you determine whether other men have done wrong or right? How do you correctly judge other men? There must be a higher authority, God.

If you choose to disobey God, the Ten Commandments, or His expectations of how to love and live life, then you must carry all the responsibility for any damage that results from your choices and actions. Whether you intended to do damage or not, you chose to disobey the expectations of the creator of everything around us; the rocks, trees, birds, animals, fish, sun, moon, solar system, even the air we breathe. What is the psychological impact of this, the mental and emotional toll? Anything you do wrong, any mistake you make in life, any damage you do to others is completely on you.

This is the greatest problem with the modern liberal, progressive mentality. It perverts the principle of freedom or free will by centering on the idea that there is no higher authority, God, over you. This is the suggestion that each person is their own god, and no person or entity has any authority over you. The problem is that no person is perfect. Everyone makes mistakes and there is no human being alive that knows everything about everyone else. This generally is how our imperfection shines brightly. In every given second or any given day our actions and words impact other people around us. Without knowing the thoughts and feelings of everyone around us we can never really know if anything we do makes a positive or negative impact on anyone else we come in contact with, even something as simple as looking someone in the eye or choosing to look away.

Without this knowledge, we can never really know if anything we do is truly right or wrong. As such, people who live their life according to the principles of the modern liberal, progressive ideology spend their lives seeking self-centered pleasure and activities that self-medicate the pain from a lifetime of guilt that continuously grows with every passing day. This leads to a lifetime of substance abuse, addiction, risky sexual behavior, depression, antisocial behaviors, and so on. This also reflects the importance of forgiveness, from God and men. People may not always forgive you, but God always will if your heart is genuine. But, you can't ask Him for forgiveness if you don't believe in Him. Now, let's get back to Eve.

In order to justify her sin, rather than admit to it, she tried to get the next person in the chain of command above her to do wrong, as this would then take the focus off her. Adam believed that eating of the fruit would please his wife, so he fell for it as well. When confronted, Adam how felt guilt as well, so he tried to shift attention to Eve rather than admit his sin and ask for forgiveness. Do you think the outcome might have been different if Adam (and/or Eve) had made the choice to admit their wrongdoing and ask God for forgiveness rather than blame someone else and sin even more? I personally think an all-powerful God could have easily started fresh with them.

Jesus said the most important rules in life are: 1) Love God with all your heart, soul, and mind, and 2) love your neighbor as yourself (Matthew 22:37-39). This is followed by the story of the Good Samaritan in which Jesus tells us that everyone around us is our neighbor, not just our family and friends. Our neighbors include the people we know as well as the people we don't. He also tells us there is no greater expression of love than a man who is willing to sacrifice his life for someone else (John 15:13). He proved His love for us in this way. He stepped into the bullet's path.

Some people do not believe Jesus was a real person, yet several historical texts from the period show that Jesus of Nazareth was, indeed, real. His life, teachings, and death are historical facts.

The Jews of Jesus's time believed that Christ would come as a great king with a great army to destroy all the enemies of the Israelites and restore their nation as rulers of the Earth. He did not come as a wealthy king but as the lowest of the low, a common carpenter's son born in a barn. His first bed was the makeshift wooden feeding trough for the goats. This required an even greater act of faith to believe in Him. Who would believe a bunch of shepherds saying angels told them of the coming of Christ? The only ones who believe are the ones who are truly seeking God. Those who desire Him are willing to listen and have faith.

In fact, there is a very simple explanation for the root of the world-wide conflict between the Jewish and Muslim worlds. Both are rooted in Old Testament history from the Holy Bible. Most Muslims consider themselves the children of Abraham, children of "The Book" (the Old Testament). Traditional Judaism and the Muslim faith believe the Messiah has not come back yet but will someday return and wipe out all the people who oppose the respective group. The Jewish leaders of Jesus's day hated Jesus of Nazareth because they believed the Messiah would lead an army against their enemies, the Romans. Muslim Jihadists today believe the Messiah will lead an army against their enemies, Israel and America. Osama Bin Laden was once thought to be this Messiah. Christians believe that God cares about all men from every nation. The enemies that the Messiah saved us from are death and hell; Jesus's sacrifice saved us from punishment for the bad things we choose to do. He saved us from ourselves, not other men.

There is no way for us to truly understand a supernatural presence that has always existed and will never end. A God powerful enough to make the Earth, outer space, and everything else in it just cannot be explained in any scientifically understandable way. We have physical evidence that dinosaurs roamed the Earth at one point. Where did they come from? There is scientific evidence to suggest a meteorite destroyed the dinosaurs. How is it that they were wiped out in a global event, but we are still here now? There is geologic evidence that now proves the polar ice caps have melted and refrozen about a dozen times since the Earth was formed. Even if we completely destroy the Earth with a global nuclear war or the polar ice caps melt and Mt. Everest becomes the new Venice Beach, God will start over. God loves everything He has created. He gave us the freedom to love Him, to love each other or destroy each other. He is not afraid of us. There is nothing we can do to destroy Him; when we attempt to destroy God, we only destroy ourselves.

Our relationship with God is not fifty-fifty. We don't deserve anything from Him. We are not equals. If we gave all our energy to worshiping and working for Him and never received anything in return, it would still be fair. God gives us anything we ask for as long as we have the faith to believe He is who He says He is. We must also have the patience to wait for the right time for God to move. Often, we are not ready for what we wish for. We should not base our choices on what we have seen others do. God's direction for you may be different from some other guy.

God's love for us is very simple, but believing it is real is very difficult. You can believe in God but still lack the faith to believe He loves you. You have to accept two things: You are a single grain of sand on the largest beach on the planet. You are one person among billions. Yet, God knows everything about you—all your desires, all your pain, all your passions. No matter what you have done, He loves you so much that He was willing to sacrifice His Son, and Jesus was willing to die, to save you from yourself, as if you were the president and He was the secret service agent that jumped in front of the bullet intended for you. We all look for happiness in life. In the process, we desire other people to give of themselves so we can be happy. However, we must be willing to give back as well. We must be willing to sacrifice for others. The best historical example of this is the life of Jesus of Nazareth.

When we love as Jesus loved, we will be hated because we care about others more than we do ourselves. Sin requires a person to love themselves first rather than love others first. Every person desires unconditional love from someone else, but most of us don't know how to give it back. This requires God's type of unconditional love, but our sinful nature doesn't allow us to embody it. No man will ever be able to love as completely and unconditionally as God does. The only way you will ever truly find happiness is to have faith in Him and try.

PARENTING: THE GREATEST INFLUENCE ON MENTAL HEALTH

THOUSANDS OF BOOKS HAVE BEEN written on parenting. If parenting can be considered a job, it is undoubtedly the most important job in the world, yet the role of a parent reaches far beyond any imaginable job description that society could come up with. At a job, you answer to an employer and perform a predetermined set of tasks to make a wage. Even if you work for yourself, you answer to customers. Someone sets a standard of expectations for you to meet, and there is a reward for meeting those expectations. You can also always change jobs if things don't work out.

As a parent, the expectations reach far beyond anything we would ever realistically consider a job. Parenting is 24/7, 365. It is a lifetime commitment that never ends. Anything and everything the child might need becomes your responsibility to provide. This includes things like food, shelter, and clothing, but it also extends into education, healthcare, and social training. More and more, we are finding that the role a parent plays in the emotional and mental development of a child is vitally important. Children learn how to handle relationships, hardships, anger, love, self-worth, accomplishments, and a range of other emotional and mental dynamics in their toddler and preschool years from mimicking the behavior that their parents model.[1]

Within every socioeconomic level, there are children who grow up to

---

1. Henslin, 2008

be successful and healthy adults. This can be said for biological families as well as blended, adoptive, and foster families. When discussing mental health in society, childhood abuse and neglect are considered the most significant contributors to mental health disorders.[2] Chemical dependency does often contribute to abuse and neglect of children, but there are also children who go on to be happy, healthy adults after growing up in chemically dependent homes. What influences determine one outcome winning out versus the other? Within the frame of reference for each of these circumstances, we often find heart-wrenching stories of abuse, neglect, and childhood mental health disorders that persist long into adult life. The circumstances of many such cases can be linked to socioeconomic status (poverty as well as affluence), family structure, chemical dependency, and other contributing circumstances.[3]

These circumstances can all contribute to the attitude and behavior of parents toward their children.[4] Throughout all circumstances a child faces, good or bad, there is one consistent influence: parents. Parental caregivers are crucial to providing a sense of safety, stability, and security in a child's life.[5] Our children's behaviors are often a reflection of our own, as our children tend to take on our own insecurities and fears[6]. Taking on the parenting role too early in life can lead to depression that then develops into a cycle of unhealthy behavior.[7] Aspects of healthy and unhealthy parenting cross all socio-economic levels and family structures. There are children who grow up in circumstances of abuse, neglect, and trauma who do not develop mental health disorders, and there are children who grow up in affluent, well-educated, nonabusive homes who do. We often take for granted the tremendous influence that caregivers have over children within these

---

2. Jenny, 2011; Wallace & Roberson, 2011
3. Wallace & Roberson, 2011
4. Desrosiers et al., 2014
5. Henslin, 2008
6. Desrosiers et al., 2014; Doba, Nandrino, Dodin & Antoine, 2014; Sandler, Wheeler & Braver, 2013
7. Desrosiers et al., 2014

circumstances. The mental health of parents is critical to their children's mental health. This is the foundation of healthy childhood development.

America struggles to understand mental health. Every discussion of school shootings, sex offenders, drug abuse, or gang violence includes the subject of mental health, but the problem is that we never really hear a lot of solutions. The first few chapters of this book were a discussion of some very universal concepts of love, faith, and freedom. This was the foundation of a happy and healthy life, the easy-to-digest milk. Now, it is time to build the house. The next several chapters were originally written as part of a college paper. The content covers a number of sensitive subjects related to mental health. As such, there are a wealth of technical concepts and research included to support the topics. This is where the hard work begins. This is the meat and potatoes of building a happy and healthy home. Some of this may be challenging to read, but I encourage you to do so with an open mind.

The purpose of including this information is to help you understand how vitally important parents are to their children. Even if you aren't a parent, you likely have relatives who have children. In many ways, your future will be dependent on the children of your friends and neighbors, and at some point in your life you will have some sort of influence on a child's life. You may be the one person who has the chance to turn someone's life around.

References to parents will include biological parents, blended families, single parents, adoptive parents, surrogates, foster parents, guardians, and designated parent unless noted otherwise. This is not the legal definition of parents; it is a reference to parents from the child's perspective. Whatever the situation is, the one or two people who are directly responsible for all of the care and attention a child would otherwise receive from parents (the care and attention a child needs and deserves), they are that child's parents.

THE IMPACT OF ABUSE AND NEGLECT

ABUSE AND NEGLECT ARE COMMON themes in mental health. Physical abuse, sexual abuse, neglect, and emotional abuse can all cause mental illness in children, and they often carry these mental illnesses into adulthood. A healthy adult may experience some challenges but has developed mentally and emotionally to the point that they can persevere through failure and try again to succeed. Traumatic brain injuries (TBI) and fetal alcohol spectrum disorder (FASD) are examples of physiological impairment to mental function. In such cases, there is a physical injury or chemical imbalance that hinders the normal development of brain tissue, leading to mental health disorders such as learning disabilities and conduct disorders. Physical and sexual abuse can lead to significant bodily injury that can damage the body's ability to function, resulting in problems with the physical development of the brain and the child's mental capacity.[8]

Within the medical community, severe physical injuries are generally defined as traumatic injuries. Traumatic injuries can lead to significant emotional damage and prolonged fear. Depression, post-traumatic stress disorder (PTSD), attachment disorders, antisocial behavior, and even developmental disorders can result from significant trauma.[9] Mental and emotional trauma can result from a wide variety of circumstances that

---

8. Jenny, 2011
9. Telles, Singh, & Balkrishna, 2012

include natural disasters, interpersonal violence, industrial accidents, fires, motor vehicle accidents, sexual assault, stranger physical assault, intimate partner violence, emotional abuse, torture, combat, terrorism, and being incarcerated in a correctional facility.[10] Trauma can contribute to lifelong mental health and substance use disorders. This may surface as the result of an incredibly destructive event, or it could also be the result of emotional distress and physical pain that occurred continuously over a prolonged period of time.

Abuse and neglect are most often associated with some sort of physical harm. This might include bruises, scars, burns, malnutrition, dirty clothes, and other visible external signs. Children who are physically abused experience serious problems including increased anxiety, poor school performance, increased aggression, lower self-esteem, impaired social problem-solving skills, high levels of behavioral problems, and psychopathology.[11] Along with significant mental health disorders, these same children often develop ongoing chemical dependencies and have regular contact with the juvenile justice system.[12] As humans, the typical perspective is to view anything that causes bodily harm or physical pain as being quantifiably worse than something that causes emotional pain. However, emotional abuse can be even more destructive than physical abuse, while neglect is considered to be the most common form of child maltreatment.[13]

The 2009 United States Department of Health and Human Services report stated an estimated 794,000 children were abused or neglected in 2007. These were only substantiated cases. The majority of these cases were for neglect, but 10.8 percent involved physical abuse. The same report suggested an estimated 1,760 children had died from abuse and neglect in 2007. The rate of abuse was almost equal for boys and girls.

---

10. Telles et al., 2012
11. McCloskey, Figueredo & Koss, 1995
12. Holt, 2001
13. Wallace & Roberson, 2011

This is particularly disturbing when you consider that most experts believe a significant percentage of abuse and neglect cases go unreported.[14]

Most of the research related to how domestic violence affects children relates to violence against the child or violence against the mother that the child may have witnessed. Many of these studies fail to consider inter-parental aggression. Mental health disorders can be the result of abuse, neglect, and hostility suffered by the child, but it can also be the result of the child witnessing their mother or an older sibling experiencing the same violence. Studies assessing the children of battered women report serious childhood problems including increased anxiety, poor school performance, conduct disorders, increased aggression, lower self-esteem, impaired social problem-solving skills, high levels of behavioral problems, and psychopathology. These results mirror those found in directly targeted children.[15] This sort of abuse within or between family members seems to have far worse affects than violence at the hands of strangers.

The hippocampus is one of the structures in the brain responsible for learning, memory, and mood. It is also one of only two structures in the brain where neurons continue to develop (neurogenesis) even into adulthood. Newborn neurons represent a very small percentage of cells in the hippocampus, and science has yet to understand exactly how neurons help to form memory and regulate mood. However, research has shown that these neurogenesis cells are vital to memory formation, learning, and behavior. Adult hippocampal neurogenesis (AHN), the formation of new neurons in the brain, is reduced by stressful experiences, and this is a contributing factor in depression-related disorders. Antidepressant therapies, including pharmacological treatments and exercise, help to increase AHN.[16] Pregnancy, the postpartum period, and maternal experiences that create high stress or trauma will reduce AHN as well. This may be associated with changes in immune system response rather than hormonal

14. Sousa et al., 2011
15. McCloskey et al., 1995
16. Anwar & Sandrine, 2012

changes and may also be a contributing factor to postpartum depression. However, exercise, activity, a micronutrient-rich diet, and an enriched environment all contribute to stimulating neurogenesis.[17]

Emotional trauma and prolonged stress can be equally destructive to both adults and children, leading to mental health disorders. Physical and sexual abuse can lead to more significant physical and emotional trauma, but physical damage is not required for a child to experience a traumatic event. Prolonged early childhood stress can hinder the development of the temporal lobe, hippocampus, and corpus callosum. This decrease in brain structures can damage the function of memory and prevent the integration of left and right brain functions. Trauma can also cause permanent changes to the pituitary, hypothalamic, and adrenal systems.[18] resulting in a crippling effect on the child's quality of life that extends into adulthood.

Descriptions of clinical signs of social deprivation in young children appeared as early as the mid-twentieth century. These descriptions include impairment to social interactions, growth, development, and immunity and were first observed in children who had been institutionalized or abused. In 1975, the first major systematic study was conducted to identify "affectional" disorders in very young children. These were children who did not receive positive affection or healthy physical contact from caregivers, and as a result they developed mental health disorders despite having access to adequate nutrition, shelter, and resources to meet other needs.[19]

Human beings have an inherent need for healthy, comforting physical contact with other people. One of the most relaxing and invigorating experiences you can have, for example, is a massage. A growing percentage of healthcare professionals consider massage to be holistic medicine. One "affectional" disorder reflected a pattern of emotionally withdrawn behavior that rarely looks for comfort, support, or protection from caregivers. When distressed, these children will become angry and lash out at

17. Anwar & Sandrine, 2012
18. Jenny, 2012; Knox, 2012
19. Gleason et al., 2011

people who attempt to offer comfort. This is known as reactive attachment disorder (RAD).[20]

These children develop highly antisocial and destructive behaviors and often experience repeated episodes of irritability, sadness, and fearfulness whether there are appropriate circumstances to support the emotions or not.[21] The child becomes intensely independent, rebellious, and often delinquent. The root cause is a repeated pattern of social neglect due to caregivers not providing for their basic emotional needs for comfort, stimulation, and affection.[22] RAD is a severe disruption of emotional and intellectual well-being that is due in large part to a lack of the basic attention, comfort, and affection that all children desire. This disorder is often the result of abuse and serious overt neglect. However, the majority of severely neglected children do not develop the disorder. If caregivers provide a high quality of care in a consistently safe environment after the child is removed from an environment of severe neglect, the disorder does not often develop. Repeated changes in caregivers can contribute to this disorder as children are shuffled from one foster care home to another or in situations where a single mother repeatedly has different boyfriends living in the home.[23]

One of the primary contributing factors to RAD is limited or no physical displays of affection and emotional support from parental figures. Further study has provided insight that children, juveniles, and adults alike have a need for basic affection and other acts that provide physical proof of emotional support and social compassion. As a result, most patients are missing a sense of long-term safety, security, and confidence in the future.[24] If acts of affection and emotional support are not consistently provided by the parents or long-term caregivers, there is no sense of reliable, consistent safety, security, and confidence for a happy and bright future. Every touch

20. American Psychiatric Association, 2013; Gleason et al., 2011
21. American Psychiatric Association, 2013; Wallace & Robertson, 2011
22. American Psychiatric Association, 2013
23. American Psychiatric Association, 2013
24. American Psychiatric Association, 2013; Wallace & Roberson, 2011

becomes a lie; every relationship seems like just another opportunity for pain. People raised with this sense of reality react to every opportunity for a relationship as if it were an attack, creating a life of antisocial behavior and emotional turmoil. This seems to be a learned behavior developed as an emotional reaction to daily recurring circumstances during childhood.[25] This behavior then develops into a parenting style used with their own children, thus passing down the disorder from generation to generation.[26]

The complexity of the circumstances that contribute to neglect include parenting styles, levels of control, levels of affection, fear, anger, and a general lack of concern for a child's basic physical and emotional needs.[27] Children don't need much to thrive. Toddlers and grade school children generally don't care how much their clothes cost or whether they eat steak or bologna. All children really want is to be warm when they are cold, have something to eat when they are hungry, and have fun. This last item seems to be the one that is most often overlooked. A child's happiness is usually dependent on the play and affection received from family.

In order for children to be healthy, they need attention and affection to know their parents care about them and reassurance that they are doing well. This is how a child develops an understanding of how to act toward and react to others. Most of us seem to understand the idea that words can hurt. As adults, we tend to develop a level of independence that helps us interpret the difference between emotional and physical pain. Normal healthy adults understand that hurt feelings won't kill you. The innocence and dependence of a child, on the other hand, create a higher level of vulnerability, making it difficult to interpret the difference between physical and emotional pain. Both become equally traumatic.

Emotional abuse can take several forms. Examples include: rejecting a child's attempts to receive attention, affection, or comfort; isolating a

25. American Psychiatric Association, 2013; Gleason et al., 2011; Sousa et al., 2011; Wallace & Roberson, 2011
26. Desrosiers et al., 2014
27. Wallace & Roberson, 2011

child by preventing the child from interacting with others; locking the child in a closet; instilling constant fear or terror in a child by threatening harm, death, or abandonment; corrupting a child by exposing the child to crime, involving the child in sexual acts, or limiting their education;[28] and failing to recognize and provide for the medical and dental health conditions that require treatment.[29] The basic need for a hug and a few kind words is equally as important as food, clothing, and shelter.

When a physical wound heals, scars often remain. Scar tissue can be tough, uncomfortable, and painful, but the body ultimately heals. It continues to function, but there is always a reminder of the injury. Abuse, neglect, and emotional trauma leave scars as well, and the emotional scars lead to symptoms that can be clinically recognized. College-age adults who experienced severe emotional maltreatment during childhood were at higher risk of suicide than those who suffered childhood physical and sexual maltreatment.[30] All of this destruction stems from "emotional" scars and rejection, not physical harm. This suggests these emotional scars always remain, just as physical scars do, but they are far more painful.

As children grow, the interaction, roles, and responsibilities within the parent-child relationship change. Toddler, preschool, and grade school children are completely dependent on parents for everything, but once children become adolescents, they experience puberty and develop their own sense of independence. As independence develops in combination with a history of abuse and neglect, teenagers often respond by rebelling against authority, parental as well as societal, leading to delinquency.[31]

Society often equates poverty with neglect and abuse. The reality, however, is that there are children who are loved and nurtured even though they live at or below the poverty level, just as there are children who live in million-dollar homes that are abused and neglected on a daily basis.

---

28. Wallace & Roberson, 2011; Wolfe & McIsaac, 2011
29. Jenny, 2011
30. Gibb et al., 2001
31. Taylor, Fritsch & Caeti, 2007; Wallace & Roberson, 2011

Abuse and neglect are found at all socioeconomic levels of society.[32] The correctional system seems to dedicate a lot of resources to treatment and tracking offenders, but we don't seem to pay nearly as much attention to the needs of the offender's children to break the vicious cycle of abuse, neglect, and mental health disorders.

32. Jenny, 2011; Taylor et al., 2007; Wallace & Roberson, 2011

PREVENTING DELINQUENCY AND
CRIMINAL BEHAVIOR

IN ITS STRICTEST INTERPRETATION, SEVERE mental illness refers to a mani-
festation of thought or mood disorders that significantly impair judgment,
behavior, the capacity to recognize reality, and the ability to cope with
the ordinary demands of life, thus causing substantial pain or disability.
Severe mental illness also refers to a wide variety of emotional needs with
functional impairments in school, family, and the community.[33] People
who experienced childhood adversities or trauma, such as learning disorders and child abuse, may be more likely to develop mental illnesses
and commit crimes. These adversities might include physical abuse,
emotional abuse, sexual abuse, neglect, bullying, and learning disorders.
Juveniles with mental illness present symptoms of moodiness; impulsive,
aggressive, and violent behavior; clinical depression; clinical psychosis;
developmental impairments; and cognitive impairments.[34] These symptoms lead to reckless and delinquent behavior.

One thing is clear: Mental health disorders are a primary contributing
factor to delinquency and crime. As the correctional population increases,
the number of mentally ill offenders will increase as well.[35]

Half of all mental health disorders have developed by the age of

---

33. Underwood, Barretti, Storms & Safonte-Strumolo, 2004
34. Bartol & Bartol, 2012b
35. Seigel, 2011; Bartol & Bartol, 2012a; Goldstein & Weiner, 2003

fourteen, but many of these childhood disorders go unnoticed.[36] Of almost one thousand juvenile offenders between the ages of fourteen and eighteen, almost 58 percent of them met the criteria for a significant mental health disorder.[37] Childhood disorders too often go untreated, leading to increasingly severe adolescent and adult mental health disorders. Juveniles sometimes turn to alcohol and other substances in an attempt to self-medicate. Of adolescents aged twelve to seventeen who reported use of an illegal substance within the past year, 32 percent also had a mental health disorder. Adolescents aged twelve to seventeen who reported a major depressive episode within the past year were also more likely to report illicit drug use as well as daily cigarette use and heavy alcohol consumption.[38]

Understanding the relationship between mental illness and offender behavior must reach beyond mental health service and treatment perspectives to look at what are traditionally referred to as "risk factors." Criminal offenders think differently than nonoffenders. Their attitudes, values, beliefs, and cognitive processing can effectively predict criminal involvement.[39] The Psychological Inventory of Criminal Thinking Skills (PICTS) is an eighty-item self-reporting tool used to measure how criminals think. It identifies eight "thinking style scales" that encapsulate the self-serving, impulsive, antisocial, and interpersonally intrusive nature of criminals' cognitive patterns.[40]

1. A tendency to blame external factors (e.g., family, social economic status, government) for one's criminal behavior.

2. Limited emotional control (e.g., "hot temper") with a propensity to maintain a "screw it" approach to dealing with problems.

36. McNamara, 2007
37. Schubert, Mulvey & Glasheen, 2011
38. McNamara, 2007
39. Morgan, Fisher, Duan, Mandracchia & Murray, 2010
40. Morgan et al., 2010

3. A sense of "ownership, privilege, and uniqueness" suggesting the belief that others (e.g., society) "owe them" and that their uniqueness affords them the right to take what they want.

4. The need for power and control.

5. A superficial concern with lack of insight regarding harm they might cause such that one's criminal behaviors are believed to be in the best interest of others.

6. A belief that they can engage in criminal acts and avoid negative consequences for their actions.

7. A lack of reasoning skills resulting in offenders taking "short-cuts" around problems.

8. A lack of direction such that offenders are easily distracted and subsequently lose sight of goals.[41]

In a national survey of adolescents, 80 percent reported consuming more than a few sips of alcohol before graduating from high school, and 55 percent reported experimenting with some sort of illicit substance.[42] Illicit substances can have a toxic effect on the body and brain development. As adolescents are still in a critical phase of emotional and cognitive development, there is good reason to believe that any substance use by adolescents can be harmful. Frequent use of illicit substances can lead to adverse behavior resulting in the risk of injury, conflict, and suspension from school. Continued use can lead to dependence, thereby creating a high risk for psychological problems, behavioral problems, depression, suicidal thoughts, risky sexual behavior, delinquency, criminal behavior, and violent behavior.[43] This is particularly significant in individuals with co-occurring substance use and mental health disorders. Those individuals have an increased risk of aggression as a result of emotional impairments

41. Morgan et al., 2010, p.331
42. Johnson, Stiffman, Hadley-Ives & Elze, 2001
43. Johnson et al., 2001

and a lack of impulse control.[44] Substance use reduces inhibitions and the self-control to resist desires to do what a person knows is wrong.

Co-occurring substance abuse and mental health disorders in adolescents is often the rule, not the exception. Adolescents who experienced severe victimization are at greater risk of co-occurring substance use and mental health disorders. Adolescents with a substance use disorder along with some type of mental health disorder are also at much greater risk of experiencing functional impairments and antisocial behaviors and are more likely to have a history of engaging in illegal activities. They are less responsive to treatment than adolescents who only have either a mental health disorder or a substance use disorder.[45]

The juvenile justice system has acknowledged the importance of family involvement in addressing the needs of youth with emotional and behavioral disorders. Parental participation, education, and support is vital to making sure that both the juvenile and their family remain engaged in the process of prevention, intervention, and aftercare.[46] The most successful treatment programs incorporate a standard list of successful treatment indicators that include: implementation of individual treatment plans, involvement of a caring adult, self-esteem building, teaching social and life skills, coordination of residential and aftercare services, family involvement, positive peer influences, implementation of a behavioral management system, community support, and creating a family-oriented environment.[47]

If mental health issues are not identified and treated early on in one's youth, they will then carry those behaviors into adulthood. Parents often resist seeking behavioral health treatment services for their children, as there are a wide range of perceptions that family secrets will be made public or that schools are trying to "brainwash" children. For the most

---

44. Grisso, 2008
45. Sabri, 2012
46. Garfinkel, 2010
47. Underwood et al., 2004

part, these perceptions are imagined based on unrealistic fears. If mental health and behavioral issues are identified early on, providing children with quality therapy can actually prevent these problems from tearing a family apart. YES, there may be times that a parent or caregiver needs a little constructive criticism to help change bad parenting behaviors, but this does not in any way suggest that parent is a bad person. In fact, it suggests the opposite; it takes strength to recognize that you can change or improve. If you do so, and it helps your family live a healthier and fuller life, you are a hero.

THE IMPACT OF NUTRITION ON
MENTAL HEALTH

THE HUMAN BODY IS AN amazingly complex organism. If bones are realigned after a break, the body will repair itself, and skin and muscle tissue operate the same way. In order for all systems to run effectively, the body requires a very delicate balance of circumstances. If this balance is not maintained, the body can be very fragile. One of these circumstances is the inclusion of the right nutrients in the blood. The heart must be able to circulate blood with just the right pressure to feed oxygen and nutrients to tissues without causing organs to rupture. Internal temperature fluctuations of just a couple degrees can shut down the body. Thus, it is no surprise that physiological changes in the body can create drastic changes in behavior.[48]

The role a parent plays in providing for the basic human needs of a child will have a significant impact on the mental health of that child, and most significantly, this applies to nutrition. Poor maternal nutrition is associated with low birth weight and cognitive abilities. It is not only the amount of food the mother consumes that is significant but also the specific types of nutrients. Maternal consumption of high levels of essential fatty acids (oily fish) and iodine, for example, are associated with higher verbal IQ and less cognitive difficulties for her child.[49] On the other hand,

48. Anwar & Sandrine, 2012; Harbottle, 2011
49. Tomlinson, Wilkinson & Wilkinson, 2009

iron deficiencies resulting in anemia are linked to cognitive impairment.[50]

The importance of maternal nutrition continues after birth as well. Several studies have suggested that breastfeeding improves cognitive ability, resulting in higher IQ scores.[51] These studies have shown that breast milk does transfer higher levels of essential fatty acids and immunoglobulins, the nutrients required for a strong immune system in infants. Mothers with strong immune systems tend to transfer this trait to their offspring through breastfeeding, and mothers with weak immune systems do the same. Poor infant nutrition can lead to slowed body growth along with impairments, both immediate and long term, to their cognitive and behavioral development.[52]

An individual with diabetes will experience significant behavioral changes as blood sugars fluctuate out of balance in one direction or the other. These behavioral changes can have a drastically negative influence on overall mental health, leading to poor decisions in managing physical health. The result can be deadly. This person must make conscious efforts to develop new behaviors and patterns of activity that will make managing their blood sugar easier and promote good mental health.[53] Good mental health is very much dependent on the presence of micronutrients that allow the brain to properly function.[54] If the rest of the body is healthy and functions properly, the mind will naturally follow.

Thiamine (B-1) is a water-soluble B vitamin required in glucose metabolism that helps brain cells convert sugar to energy.[55] When this element is missing, the brain cells cannot produce the energy to function properly. The simple processing of whole grains and brown rice into white flour and white rice removes much of the nutritional value of these building blocks of life. Understanding this process led to the breakthrough

---

50. Tomlinson et al., 2009
51. Tomlinson et al., 2009
52. Tomlinson et al., 2009
53. Lloyd, 2010
54. Harbottle, 2011
55. Isenberg-Grzeda, Kutner & Nicolson, 2012

in human biology and the discovery of Wernicke-Korsakoff syndrome, a deficiency of thiamine that causes disorientation and memory loss.[56]

In most industrialized countries, processed foods are fortified. This refers to the process of adding additional vitamins and other nutrients to foods (e.g., cereal, breads, and snacks) as they are manufactured. Even in industrialized countries where foods are fortified with additional thiamine, healthy people typically consume an average of 0.4 to 2 mg a day.[57] 1.5 mg is the average recommended daily supplement, but this is far less than the overall recommended daily allowance that the body needs. Alcohol abuse, AIDS, cancer, chronic infections, eating disorders, and other immunity disorders can all potentially develop into Wernicke-Korsakoff syndrome.[58]

Omega-3 fatty acids from oily fish help lower the potential for depression. They are a structural component of cell membranes and play an important role in our central nervous system function and vision. Vitamin D is vital to overall health, including bone growth and cognitive function. Vitamin D deficiency contributes to a greater risk of depression, bipolar disorder, and schizophrenia. Besides being the best source of omega-3 fatty acids, fish is also the best source of vitamin D.[59] Studies of omega-3 fatty acids, folate, zinc, thiamin, and vitamin D all show that they help reduce the risk of depression.[60]

Folate, vitamin B6, and vitamin B12 each play an important role in the development of neurotransmitters in the brain. Vitamin B6 helps the body control plasma homocysteine concentrations that reduce the risk of vascular disease and cognitive disorders that occur as we get older. Vitamin B12 is vital to the development of S-adenosyl methionine that in turn allows for the development of neurotransmitters. A vitamin B12 deficiency is associated with memory loss, depression, and cognitive dysfunction. Contrastingly, high levels of B12 and folate are associated with

56. Isenberg-Grzeda et al., 2012; Zubaran, Fernandes & Rodnight, 1997
57. Isenberg-Grzeda et al., 2012
58. Isenberg-Grzeda et al., 2012; Zubaran et al., 1997
59. Dog, 2010
60. Harbottle, 2011

positive outcomes in antidepressant therapy.[61]

Iron deficiency has been proven to cause fatigue, apathy, and poor concentration. Reduced iron intake may also inhibit neurotransmitter development and function. Zinc is vital to cell metabolism throughout the body, particularly in immune system function. Magnesium is a crucial component in over three hundred biochemical processes in the body. It helps maintain normal heart rhythm and blood pressure along with normal muscle function, nerve function, and a healthy immune system. Magnesium is also important to regulating blood sugar and bone density. Insufficient magnesium levels can contribute to restless leg syndrome, agitation, irritability, sleep disorders, and depression.[62]

Anwar & Sandrine (2012) gathered research from more than one hundred nutritional studies to develop an understanding of the effects that various nutrients have on neurogenesis, the constant rebuilding of brain cells. The neuroreceptor brain cells carry electrical impulses throughout the brain, allowing for the transmission of thoughts, memories, and emotions. Fruits, vegetables, fish, and other natural foods rich in omega-3 fatty acids and other micronutrients were found to be most beneficial to neurogenesis and overall health. It was not surprising that several studies proved a high-sugar, high-fat, and high-calorie diet was detrimental to neurogenesis, contributing to depression, mood disorders, and reduced cognitive function.[63] Calories are the body's fuel. We need fuel for our body to generate the energy needed to operate. However, the body is robbed of nutrients and systems slow down as excessive calories are processed as waste.

Refined sugars in beverages and processed foods digest easily and are absorbed by the body quickly, causing blood sugar spikes.[64] This causes a sudden increase in insulin, leading to an adverse drop in blood sugar later.

---

61. Dog, 2010
62. Dog, 2010
63. Anwar & Sandrine, 2012
64. Harbottle, 2011; Lloyd, 2010

This fluctuation can lead to hypoglycemia, and this can lead to increased risk of diabetes.[65] Sugar can have a significant negative impact on blood glucose control and serotonin levels, making sugar a scientifically proven contributor to depression.[66]

Caffeine in small amounts was found to increase neurogenesis, but the neurons did not survive for very long.[67] Caffeine and alcohol are diuretics, leading to the potential for dehydration. Dehydration can be deadly, but even slight dehydration can lead to restlessness, irritability, and diminished cognitive capacity. High levels of caffeine can lead to sleep deprivation, high blood pressure, anxiety, and mood disorders.[68] The incredible complexity of the human body allows for the various systems to work together to nourish the body, flush out toxins, fight disease, and heal after injuries. Even so, the ability to do so is still based on a very delicate balance of circumstances that can be drastically disrupted by small things we often overlook and take for granted.

Processed foods are often high in saturated fats and trans fats. As natural foods are processed in a factory, the raw ingredients are sent through extensive preservation processing that often destroys the majority of the micronutrients essential for the body. A diet that consists mostly of prepackaged processed food will not provide young bodies with the nutrients they need, leading to depression, mood swings, and other mental disorders.[69] This is even more destructive for children than adults. People who experience depression and other mental health disorders often lose interest in making an effort to shop for food and prepare meals, and this naturally leads to an even greater reliance on processed foods. The result is an increased problem managing nutritional intake, weight control, blood sugar, and chemical imbalances in the body.[70] In spite of the fortification

65. Dog, 2010
66. Harbottle, 2011; Lloyd, 2010
67. Anwar & Sandrine, 2012
68. Harbottle, 2011
69. Harbottle, 2011
70. Harbottle, 2011

of processed foods, the natural state of the food that we eat is still far superior to processed convenience foods. The essential vitamins, minerals, antioxidants, proteins, and other building blocks of life can easily be cooked out in the processing and preservation process.

The capacity for the human body to maintain a strong cardiovascular system, fight cancer, resist disease, and increase longevity is largely dependent on a nutritional diet and regular activity and exercise. A diet rich in micronutrients is as important to mental health as it is to physical health. This is particularly important in childhood development but also extends into adulthood.[71] Multiple studies have suggested that a diet consisting of whole foods reduces the risk of depression significantly, whole foods being fruits, vegetables, whole grains, nuts, legumes, fish, and a small amount of wine. Observational studies in the 1950s noted that people following a Mediterranean-style diet had significantly lower rates of heart disease and cancer than other populations. Their life expectancies were longer than other groups as well. On average, 35 percent of the calories in Mediterranean diets are derived from fats. However, the majority of this is fish oils and olive oil.[72]

Most children have experienced the dread of being forced to eat their vegetables at dinnertime. As it turns out, this dread is often for good reason, as many people choose to overcook or under season their vegetables. A good glaze of butter, a little salt, a little pepper, and maybe even a little honey can change the vegetable eating experience altogether. For decades, self-appointed health experts told us that butter, salt, and oil were all bad for us,[73] but science has now proven that many of the substances we know are unhealthy in large amounts can be beneficial in small amounts. Examples would be salt, red wine, beer, dark chocolate, and butter. Red wine, for instance, is high in antioxidants. Many doctors recommend drinking one glass of wine a day. People with substance use disorders, however, will

71. Anwar & Sandrine, 2012
72. Dog, 2010
73. Harbottle, 2011

use this as an excuse to drink more. This is the mentality that says, "If one glass is good, then three glasses must be even better, right?"

No! One glass is enough.

The problem with alcohol is not necessarily the substance itself; this is a problem of inhibited self-control in the individual. Medicines from opiates and other natural plant substances are essential for treating injuries, disease, and promoting healing, but these same substances can be addictive and destructive if the amounts are not precisely controlled. Alcohol addiction can be destructive as well, but that does not change the fact that very small amounts of wine or beer can contribute to good health. People who suggest that a certain substance is to blame for a person's struggles in life are often the individuals who struggle with their own limited capacity for self-regulation and self-control.

Omega-3 fatty acids, tryptophan, and folate are just three of the dietary nutrients associated with the prevention of mental health disorders, including ADHD, autism, depression, and psychosis. Concentration, academic achievement, and behavior can all be improved when children do not miss breakfast and eat a nutritional lunch.[74] Some might say this lends support for school lunch and breakfast programs, but what about dinnertime, weekends, and meals over summer vacation? School and community programs will never be an effective substitute for active, healthy parenting.

The relationship between food and mental health reaches much deeper than just nutrition. Hunger is the basic desire for food. Hunger may also describe the limited availability of food. Food insecurity is the limited ability to understand how to find and maintain adequate amounts of food or quality food in socially acceptable ways.[75] This typically involves a limited understanding of what is required to provide adequate nutrition for a healthy and active lifestyle. Food insecurity is associated with obesity, diabetes, heart disease, hypertension, depression, and malnutrition. It often has nothing to do with limited access to food; rather, it is a limited

74. Tomlinson et al., 2009
75. Strike, Rudzinski, Patterson & Millson, 2012

understanding of nutrition and health. Food insecurity combined with substance abuse can lead to significant health problems such as vitamin deficiencies, anemia, observable emaciation, low body mass, tooth decay, gastrointestinal distress, and a variety of other physiological ailments. A proven link exists between food insecurity, AIDS/HIV, and sexually transmitted diseases, as food insecurity is directly associated with risky behaviors like having unprotected sex.[76]

Nutrition is absolutely crucial to raising physically and mentally healthy children. Children need these essential vitamins, minerals, and micronutrients for their continued development. They need high levels of carbohydrates, proteins, fats, fiber, and water as well. All of these elements work together to allow the body to generate energy, and this provides the body with the materials needed for growth. Whole grains, fruits, vegetables, fresh meats, and other whole foods will provide this nutritional balance much better than processed foods. Microwave-ready foods will never be adequate substitutes for meals prepared with fresh whole foods. This has nothing to do with the microwave being some sort of evil device; as a matter of fact, the majority of microwave-ready foods already lost much of their nutritional value before they made it to the store. The unfortunate reality is that many parents don't provide the basics of nutrition for their children. This may be due to misconceptions of nutrition, unhealthy eating habits, food insecurity, or even something as simple as a lack of cooking skills. It is difficult to imagine how something as simple as providing food can be a challenge. To combat this, parents must understand that high-quality nutrition is vital to their child's physical and mental health.

---

76. Strike et al., 2012

EMOTIONAL AND INTELLECTUAL
NEEDS OF CHILDREN

BASIC INTERACTION BETWEEN A PARENT/CAREGIVER and their child is incredibly important in development. The majority of interaction is based on simple acts of encouragement or discouragement that occur in daily activities, such as household tasks. Children are eager to learn. Children desire praise for doing things well as we all do, but young children have not yet developed the motor skills or reasoning needed to figure things out on their own. They need us to help them understand basic tasks, and adults often fail to see the world through the innocence of a child. We often fail to realize that simple parental verbal and nonverbal interaction can encourage or discourage a child's social development.[77] There is a basic inherent human desire in all of us to receive the attention, time, and affection of others. The importance of parents spending time interacting with their children cannot be overlooked. This can be play, reading, chores, or hobbies, and the quantity of those activities is significantly less important than the quality of the interactions. For children, work can be just as satisfying as play when quality interaction is provided.

Developing good patterns of behavior is important to good mental health in balancing emotional response to circumstances you face in daily life. This includes making good choices, the ability to resist the impulse to do something unhealthy out of personal gratification. Behaviors, emotional

---

77. Grebelsky-Lichtman, 2014; Yoo & Huang, 2013

responses, and impulse control are all functions of the brain.[78] Children and adolescents who developed strong bonds of attachment to parents were far less likely to develop antisocial behavior patterns. Preventing child abuse and domestic violence by encouraging healthy parent-to-child attachment should translate to less antisocial behavior. With that being said, encouraging healthy attachments between child and parent after significant exposure to abuse and violence at an early age may not be enough to counteract the impact of trauma already experienced by the child.[79]

Research consistently shows that the quality of parenting from both mothers and fathers is important to the well-being of a child. Children who are exposed to abuse and domestic violence do not develop relationships with parents as strong as children who are not, and levels of attachments did not differ based on a child's exposure to one form of abuse and violence over another.[80] In one study, parents and their children were observed playing a game. As the child had difficulty operating controls or choosing what to do during play, parents' responses were recorded along with the child's reactions. The parent-child interactions were separated into four categories: 1) Parent was apathetic, uninterested in helping the child with the game. 2) Parent was verbally harsh with the child. 3) Parent was verbally encouraging with the child while being unhelpful or took the controller from the child to complete the task. 4) Parent encouraged the child to keep trying and gave directions to complete the task while allowing the child to work the controller and finish the task.[81]

The interactions described in the first two categories were obviously destructive to the parent-child interaction. Category three, giving encouraging words praising the child without providing actual assistance or taking over the game, resulted in uncooperative behavior from the child. However, verbally challenging words that corrected and directed the child

---

78. Harbottle, 2011
79. Sousa et al., 2011
80. Sousa et al., 2011
81. Grebelsky-Lichtman, 2014

combined with nonverbal actions that helped the child operate the controls and complete the task correctly on their own resulted in cooperative behavior from the child.[82] This is the interaction described in category four. Children desire correction and direction, as long as this is provided in a loving manner. They don't need you to do everything for them; they need you to teach them how to do everything.

If Mom takes a toy away and places it on top of a shaky bookcase, the child's only thought is to climb up and get it. A child has not developed any sense of whether the bookcase is strong enough to climb or what could happen if the piece of furniture falls on top of them. This limit of understanding does not indicate that there is something wrong. Childhood is a process of mental development. Children must start with 2+2=4 before they can understand how to multiply fractions. Children have a desire to learn and explore, and as they do, their minds and hearts develop. Much of this is based on experience, and this development occurs emotionally as well.

Children are still learning about life, love, and relationships. Mental health issues can disrupt the ability to learn how to develop positive relationships and become happy, healthy, productive adults.[83] For instance, a child doesn't understand that thunder during a storm can't hurt you. The natural comfort and reassurance that everything is ok is found in a hug, a soft voice, and some comforting words of reassurance. Most of the time, a four year old child will react to a stranger's greeting by clinging to a parent's leg or hiding behind the parent. The desire for protection and shelter is a natural reaction to uncertain circumstances.

Almost every child has experienced a skinned knee while learning to ride a bike. The usual reaction is to stop learning for fear of more pain. In order to overcome this, a compassionate adult must help the child understand that this is part of this learning process. The child needs reassurance that the pain from a skinned knee will go away. A hug and a few words of

82. Grebelsky-Lichtman, 2014
83. Sandler et al., 2013; Sousa et al., 2011; Yoo & Huang, 2013

comfort help the child know that the pain is normal and temporary. This child needs help getting up, cleaning off the wound, and encouragement to try again until success is experienced. If the child is allowed to stop trying because of pain, fear, or embarrassment, the child will not experience the thrill of success! This will create challenges as the child progresses into adolescence and adulthood. It may sometimes be healthy to stop trying for today. If a young lion tries to attack a zebra and gets kicked in the leg, he can't run, can't fight, and the zebra will get away. Having learned a valuable lesson about zebras, the lion will change his tactics. Eventually, he will master stalking and killing a zebra. Similarly, the child must keep trying, and the parent must keep helping them until success is achieved.

If the parent's response in this situation is to say, "Stop crying, what's wrong with you?" or "You can't do something simple like this? Get up and stop whining!" then this child will not learn to manage fear and pain in a healthy way. Harsh words that make the child feel stupid or embarrassed just add to the pain. What is left is a child who becomes angry easily and recoils from an adult's attempt to offer kindness or comfort.[84]

Parents must be emotionally and intellectually healthy if they hope to adequately provide for the emotional and intellectual needs of their children. The home environment must be healthy and safe in order to provide the best opportunity for development. Depression in parents can be a powerfully destructive force. Maternal depression can result in attachment disorders and insecurity. They have difficulty making behavioral and emotional adjustments to changing circumstances. This can begin when the child is as young as six months old. Paternal depression often does not influence children until eighteen months of age as fine motor skills begin to develop.[85] Alcohol, tobacco, toxins (lead, street drugs), and even high stress can lead to low birth weight and even premature birth. Babies with low birth weight are often at higher risk of developing infections, as they already face challenges to physical development. They tend to have lower

84. American Psychiatric Association, 2013
85. For-Wey, Bih-Ching, Tung-Liang & Shio-Jean, 2009

IQ scores along with greater difficulty in language and reading skills as children.[86]

Education is important to fostering good mental health. Educated parents will pass on the importance of education to their children, thus creating greater opportunities for healthy childhood development and good mental health.[87] These parents are more likely to spend time reading books to their children, playing games with them, and generally spending time with them. They will spend more time taking them to the library and spend more time at school events even though they often work more hours in a week than less-educated parents. Healthy parents practice better parenting practices that include self-control, consistent discipline, less irritability, and less aggression.[88] You don't need a college degree to be a good parent, but you do need to do everything in your power to give your children a desire to learn.

Religious beliefs, or lack thereof, are generally established in cultural circles within the family. Human spirituality and religious beliefs can be very difficult to measure. Life behind bars in particular can be very emotionally challenging. Eytan (2011) collected the results of twelve studies related to spirituality and mental health within prison populations. Participants were interviewed to compare their opinions against the accompanying rates of clinical depression and disciplinary incidents. The study proved that spirituality has a significant impact on depression and behavior.[89] Many would suggest that this is a reflection of all aspects of the human experience, the suggestion that a person's faith in a higher authority gives hope, peace, and resilience.

Understandably, spirituality is difficult to quantify. Throughout the centuries, spirituality has served to set societal standards for morality, human interaction, respect for each other, and respect for creation. As

---

86. Tomlinson et al., 2009
87. Yamauchi, 2010; For-Wey et al., 2009
88. Yamauchi, 2010
89. Eyton, 2011

separation of church and state has been twisted and special interest groups will not allow prayer in school, we have observed a not-so-unrelated increase in juvenile delinquency and teen pregnancy. If spirituality can serve to reduce violence and depression in prison environments, parents might take note to try and seek the same influence at home.

CONFLICT AND DIVORCE (BREAKING UP AND BLENDING FAMILIES)

CONFLICT IS AN UNAVOIDABLE PART of life. In most families, the adults argue about a variety of things, and this arguing is often overlooked as something children wouldn't understand. We choose to believe that the arguments or abuse that go on behind closed doors do not affect them. This is not the case at all. The real challenge to effective and compassionate parenting occurs in life's difficulties. A child's sense of long-term safety and security is very much determined by the stability of their parent's relationship. This stability, or lack thereof, is then reflected in the parent's relationship with the child. It can be very difficult to differentiate between poor parenting and emotional neglect,[90] but constant family conflict is considered a form of emotional abuse.

Physical abuse and sexual abuse are easily identifiable as emotionally traumatic events. We don't often realize that emotional abuse can come in many forms, all of which have an equally destructive impact on a child's life. Children who are physically abused experience serious childhood problems including increased anxiety, poor school performance, conduct disorders, increased aggression, lower self-esteem, impaired social problem solving skills, high levels of behavioral problems, and psychopathology. The sad reality is that children of battered women experienced the same serious emotional and developmental problems as their mothers

90. Wolfe & McIsaac, 2011

123

even when they were not the target of the abuse.[91]

In many cases, parents have a limited awareness of what is actually going on in their child's life. Parents perceive and judge events very differently than their children do.[92] Many parents don't understand how their children feel about even commonplace events that occur; a child often struggles with basic day-to-day challenges in life that adults are used to and take for granted. This leads us to the question of measuring stress in children.

Stress can also be measured biologically in children, providing biological evidence of ongoing stress they are experiencing. Cortisol is released into the body through the hypothalamus-pituitary-adrenal (HPA) axis in anticipation of or during stressful encounters.[93] This allows the body to respond to conflict, stress, and violence with higher energy levels, and it is an automatic physiological response to the mind's perception of stress. As such, measuring the chemical composition that results from this process provides a significant measure of prolonged stress. Cortisol can be found in blood, urine, saliva, and hair, and these measurements provide researchers with biological evidence of chronic stress to support the perceptions of children. Physiological effects of stress can also be measured biologically by studying brain function, cardiovascular functions, and immune system responses.[94]

Prolonged traumatic and stressful events in a child's life may severely affect the physiological and psychological health of children, leading to depression or other mental health disorders as they grow into adolescents and adults. This is the direct result of neurobiological changes, cardiovascular stress, or autoimmune diseases and often presents in stressed children as headaches, stomach pain, and tiredness.[95] The way a child perceives life events seems to have a significant impact on their behavior and adjustment

91. McCloskey et al., 1995
92. Vanaelst, De, Huybrechts, Rinaldi & De, 2012
93. Vanaelst et al., 2012
94. Vanaelst et al., 2012
95. Vanaelst et al., 2012

to the events. Perception may include the child's understanding of why it happened, who is to blame, the child's influence over the events, and the child's perception of how others feel about the event or themselves.[96]

The long-term mental health implications of stress reach far into adulthood. Hopelessness theory suggests that childhood maltreatment and other negative childhood events lead to an overall negative view of life, a cognitive process based on negative views of consequences and self-implications of stressful life events. This leads to hopelessness, depression, and thoughts of suicide. Hopelessness is also the most common predictor of suicide in adolescents and adults, including the elderly.[97] Adults who suffered significant emotional maltreatment during childhood were at higher risk of suicide ideation than those who suffered childhood physical and sexual maltreatment.[98] Emotional abuse and neglect during childhood was more likely to contribute to adult depression than childhood physical or sexual abuse.[99] Developing supportive social circles, effective life skills, and problem solving skills are key to reducing hopelessness.[100] All of this would seem to suggest that emotional neglect and maltreatment can be even more destructive to mental health than physical or sexual abuse.

Couples divorce for many reasons—infidelity, stress, finances, illness, and so on. These are often the worst situations for families to go through, especially children. These often lead to legal conflicts involving prolonged court battles related to finances, personal property, and custody. High-conflict divorce involves intense arguing, verbal abuse, anger, shouting, and stress.[101] A child's description of conflict between parents leading up to a divorce was shown to predict their resulting psychological symptoms. The child's interpretation of the reason for the problems between the parents played a significant role as well. The frequency,

---

96. Vanaelst et al., 2012
97. Bhar & Brown, 2011; 2012
98. Gibb et al., 2001
99. Powers, Ressler & Bradley, 2009
100. Bhar & Brown, 2011; 2012
101. Sandler et al., 2013

intensity, content, and resolution of interparental conflict determined the child's understanding of why parents were fighting. Children often believe they are the reason parents are fighting, and parents often underestimate children's sensitivity to conflict.[102]

Research suggests parental conflict and poor maternal or paternal parenting can be mediated by the quality of parenting provided by the other parent. Two quantitative factors related to this quality of parenting were the amount of time spent with and a higher number of overnight stays with the healthy parent.[103] Research consistently shows that the quality of parenting from both the mother and father is important to the well-being of a child. As such, most court-related parent education programs teach the importance of both parents to the post-divorce adjustment plan, but they often fail to take into account the context that determines the quality of the parent-child relationship.[104] The courts will take into account psychological issues related to the well-being of the children, but they are often powerless to impact the attitude parents have regarding the impact their behavior has on the mental health of their children. The subtle impacts of hostility in family relationships cannot be overemphasized.

Parents often underestimate their children's sensitivity to conflict, and indirect emotional abuse during childhood can have a destructive impact on an adult's interactions with their family members as well. The majority of women who perpetrated intimate partner violence had witnessed the actions of a physically aggressive mother as children. Early in life, they were taught that it is acceptable for women to use violence to resolve conflict.[105] Maternal parenting behavior can help mediate the effect that domestic violence has on externalized behavioral problems as children enter their grade school years.[106] However, aggressive maternal behavior can also have a destructive impact.

---

102. McCloskey et al., 1995
103. Sandler et al., 2013
104. Sandler et al., 2013
105. Babcock, Miller & Siard, 2003
106. Yoo & Huang, 2013

Maternal parenting was measured by the mother's behavior toward the child as well as the mother's use of physical discipline. Destructive maternal parenting was identified as mothers being unresponsive to the child's emotional state and emotional needs, harsh toward the child during stressful circumstances, or lacking verbal and/or social skills when interacting with the child.[107] Discipline is important for the mental health of both child and parent. However, the excessive use of physical discipline was the single greatest detriment to the mediating effect of maternal mental health on externalized behavior problems.[108]

Excessive discipline can become abusive. However, the opposite can be destructive as well. Parent abuse is a form of family violence where children abuse or manipulate their parents. Male and female children can be equally abusive toward parents, but the type of abuse will differ between them. Mothers are usually the targets of this type of abuse; parent abuse is more common in maternal single-parent homes. Children are more likely to abuse their parents when the parents are overly permissive or use inconsistent rules and consequences.[109] Children in overly permissive homes tend to have trouble controlling their emotions and impulses, and this also makes them more likely to engage in risky behavior like substance abuse and sexual promiscuity.[110]

In order for children to find a healthy sense of safety and stability in life, they need relationships they can depend on. For the courts and social services, the majority of the focus is on maternal parenting rather than paternal parenting. However, research has shown that fathers play a crucial role in their children's lives and development as well. There is a serious lack of attention given to fathers in regard to therapy and child protection.[111] One significant difference in high-violence sex offenders as compared to low-violence sex offenders and the general population was

107. Yoo & Huang, 2013
108. Yoo & Huang, 2013
109. Kennair & Mellor, 2007
110. Wolfe & McIsaac, 2011
111. Ferguson, 2012

a lack of significant male relationships that provided experience or a perception of social support. These violent sex offenders came from families in which fathers and other sources of male relationships were rarely available and offered no emotional attention.[112] Many therapists avoid working with fathers out of fear for their own protection and a lack of confidence in their capacity to provide effective services. Fathers are also ignored because of perceptions, whether true or false, of danger, recklessness, or a general belief that lower-class working men can't or don't care. In spite of these beliefs of paternal abuse, the vast majority of research proves that most fathers do, in fact, care. More importantly, paternal influence and involvement is a good thing for children.[113]

Many of the factors that place children at risk of mental health disorders are the same contributing stressors facing teen parents. These include a lack of financial and material resources, inconsistent housing, and a lack of social support.[114] Adolescence is a developmental stage wherein the body is still developing along with the intellect. The majority of our growth involving our sense of individualism, identity, and ability to develop healthy interpersonal relationships takes place during the teen years of adolescence.[115] As such, this can be an emotionally stressful time, leading to the potential for unhealthy development. Adolescence and young adulthood is a critical time for learning how to develop romantic relationships as well. Attachment disorders often create challenges in practicing healthy communication along with little emotional satisfaction between partners. These stressors combined with the stress of pregnancy can lead to significant risk of serious depression in adolescent and young adult couples, placing themselves at risk along with the mental health of their children.[116]

Mental health disorders that are not the result of external physiological

112. Gutiérrez-Lobos et al., 2001
113. Ferguson, 2012
114. Desrosiers et al., 2014
115. Desrosiers et al., 2014
116. Desrosiers et al., 2014

factors (e.g., TBI, FASD, physical injuries, birth defects, and malnutrition) are often the result of harm stemming from unhealthy family relationships.[117] Prevention of abuse and neglect that leads to mental health disorders is dependent on parental awareness and education to help new parents understand the emotional sensitivity and needs of children. Parents must understand the fact that conflict and hostility will happen within families, especially as hardships arise and children develop into puberty. Effective parenting, however, is dependent on a desire to meet the physical and emotional needs of the child with compassion that sees a balance between the child's perspective and the parent's perspective. Children don't need everything they want, but they don't need everything you want either.

We often view raised voices as a sign of hostility. In many minority cultures, it is important to have the extended family stay together under the same roof, and the fact is that families that contain elderly members often must talk louder in order for the family to communicate. This may also be the case in families of industrial workers who gradually lose their hearing due to their working conditions. In such cases, our external perceptions of hostility within family relations can be quite wrong, and the opposite could be true as well. A very quiet and polite family environment may be a sign of significant broken relationships and control issues. The nature of family relationships is such that there will inevitably be conflict at times. Healthy development is not dependent on having no conflict; it is dependent on learning how to resolve conflict in a respectful and caring manner.[118] A healthy family environment requires more than just putting food on the plate, a warm house, and clean clothes. These are all important, but children also require tenderness, compassion, guidance, stability, play, and peace in the house to be truly healthy.

---

117. Desrosiers et al., 2014; Henslin, 2008; Jenny, 2011; McCloskey et al., 1995; Sandler et al., 2013; Vanaelst et al., 2012; Wallace & Roberson, 2011
118. McCloskey et al., 1995; Vanaelst et al., 2012; Wolfe & McIsaac, 2011

SUBSTANCE ABUSE IN FAMILIES

THERE IS NO QUESTION THAT substances like alcohol, marijuana, opiates, prescription drugs, illicit drugs, and even caffeine can have a powerfully addictive and destructive effect. These effects can be destructive to people's lives. However, there are certain facts that cannot be ignored: Most adolescents are not likely to experience adverse consequences for experimenting with illicit substances.[119] In considering this, we must realize that alcohol, marijuana, and other substances are not necessarily the greatest contributing factor to substance abuse and mental health disorders; negative social factors are. These negative social factors include associations with peers who use or tolerate substance use, parental influence, and other community or school-related social influences. Peer-to-peer influence is not as significant as was once thought, but the influence of role models most certainly is. Substance use and dependence within the family is the greatest predictor of adolescent substance use.[120]

This helps to explain the recurring cycle of addiction and mental health disorder in families with instances of long-term chemical dependence. Substance abuse is often a contributing factor to domestic abuse, including child abuse and neglect, not only in regard to direct abuse of a child while under the influence of a substance but also as a contributing

119. Johnson et al., 2001
120. Johnson et al., 2001

131

factor to fetal defects and developmental disorders. A wide range of physiological or psychological impairments can result from maternal substance use, before, during, and after pregnancy.[121]

Children look up to their parents. They will naturally mimic what adults do in an effort to gain attention and please their parents by doing what they do. Children are influenced by what they see others do, not by what they are told to do. Experts believe people use the psychotropic effects of drugs to cope with the emotional distress of psychiatric disorders, leading to addiction.[122] Mothers of addicts and alcoholics experience a high level of emotional over-involvement along with high emotional reactivity to the child.[123] The parents' behavior tends to transfer depression and insecurity from the parent to child, leading to intergenerational addictive behaviors.

Chemical dependency and mental health disorders are often viewed as two different problems, but research has proven that it is not effective to attempt to treat one type of disorder separate from the other.[124] This is one of the most significant revelations within mental health in recent years. Most organizations are not equipped to treat both chemical dependency and psychiatric or depression disorders at the same time, but treatment must include all known chemical dependency and psychiatric disorders in order to be truly effective.[125] Finding a solution to this problem is not easy. Chemical dependency treatment models such as AA have traditionally been much more confrontational than mental health treatment models. Mental health treatment models are based more on being supportive, leading to unproductive, almost conflicting treatment methods. Given the nature of chemical dependency treatment, there is great resistance to pharmacological treatments that can be very effective in mental health treatment and helpful in chemical dependency treatment as well.[126]

121. Jenny, 2011
122. Brady & Sinha, 2005
123. Doba et al., 2014
124. Sterling et al., 2011
125. Sterling et al., 2011
126. Sterling et al., 2011

The most successful treatment outlines for co-occurring chemical dependency and mental health disorders require a lot of supervision through the accompanying activities and counseling. Cognitive behavioral therapy (CBT) is important in helping the patient understand how their behavior impacts their relationships, jobs, and other areas of life.[127] This allows for the opportunity to develop healthy behaviors to replace the destructive ones. However, changing behavior is not enough. The fact of the matter is that the pain, fears, and anguish from trauma continue on long after the trauma ends. During that time, there will be an increase in emotional sensitivity that will drive a greater desire to medicate the pain with the substance of choice. This requires extensive supervision and activities to distract from the desire for the substance.[128]

Family therapy is more effective than individual therapy in treating substance use disorders. Social support is a large contributing factor to the outcome of therapy. Oftentimes, there are problems within the family interactions or relationships that contribute to substance use disorders. Family therapy provides the opportunity for the family to work through these problems together, leading to a healthier outcome. The majority of clients with less severe disorders naturally select family therapy, resulting in a greater number of effective sessions taking place in fewer sessions when compared to individual or mixed therapy.[129]

The impact that family has on social influence and adolescent behavior reaches beyond the direct influence of the parent's behavior. Alcohol and drug abuse is often common in adults under the supervision of the correctional system. Mental health disorders are three time more likely in correctional populations than in the general population,[130] and substance abuse is one of the most significant disorders in this population. This suggests that there are a significant number of mentally ill criminal offenders

127. Telles et al., 2012
128. Telles et al., 2012
129. Morgan, Crane, Moore & Eggett, 2013
130. Louden, Skeem, Camp & Christensen, 2008

in our communities who are living with families and raising their children. In many cases, parents attempt to change from negative social behavior to pro-social behavior in an effort to improve the influence they have on their children. This decision is born out of concern for the child's ultimate outcome. However, that parent will usually experience a negative response from their own social environment, which is then observed by the adolescent. As a result, the adolescent will not always follow the path set forth by the parent out of fear of rejection from social influences.[131]

The social support, perceptions of safety, love, structure, and basic sense of stability in life that come from a healthy family environment may be the most important contributing factor to any aspect of human development and overall mental health. Even in relation to the treatment of substance use and mental health disorders, efforts to change the family environment from one exhibiting unhealthy circumstances and behaviors to healthy ones seem to have the greatest contributing factor to overcoming mental health and substance use disorders.

---

131. Bartol & Bartol, 2012a

CREATING HEALTHY FAMILIES

CULTURAL SHIFTS IN ASPECTS OF modern life seem to be causing higher levels of anxiety and depression, especially in young people. Social changes have created an overall culture in which individualism is emphasized, resulting in an increase in mental health disorders. The "California Self" requires perfection from others in personal and work relationships while emphasizing the need to be independent from, not dependent on, others. This creates increased social isolation as well as higher performance expectations that people place on each other.[132]

As this new sense of individualism develops in our culture, social connections become weak, loneliness increases, and depression thrives. Research has found that juvenile suicide rates are higher in cultures that emphasis individualism.[133] The late 1980s and early 1990s became something of a social low point in the US. Suicide rates in young people and violent crime rates reached historic highs. The number of people living alone and the number of infants born to unmarried parents were high as well, indicating that society was at a point of social disconnection. Divorce rates were decreasing, but so were marriage rates.[134]

The two key aspects of effective citizenship include understanding the law and playing by the rules. Unfortunately, many citizens do not receive

132. Twenge, 2011
133. Twenge, 2011
134. Twenge, 2011

an education in the law until they become involved in the criminal justice system. In many low-socioeconomic communities, this is their only education in the law, leading to negative perceptions of government.[135] Many adolescents are given negative perceptions of the police and criminal justice system as a result of family members and peers who had prior negative experiences of their own.[136] These facts suggest that the majority of criminal or delinquent behavior develops as a process of influence and learning from the people we are close to: our family and peers.[137]

Community revitalization programs over the last decade or so focused on cleaning up the appearance of low-socioeconomic neighborhoods. This did not address the real problems at the core, however, including minimal employment opportunities, low parental involvement, low parental supervision, and limited education. This reflects the influence that parenting has on issues of delinquency, risky behavior, and gang participation. A child's sense of safety at home is often viewed as primarily relating to abuse or neglect.[138] From a child's perspective, simple things like a parent showing interest in a creative project or a willingness to read a book together before bed can play a significant role in the child's perception of safety.[139] Understanding this is only a small part of the battle. The capacity for outside organizations to have any influence over parenting behavior is limited and often does not occur until there is a report and evidence of physical abuse or severe neglect.[140]

The issues of race and ethnicity are steadily becoming less significant in regard to understanding gang membership. The circumstances that determined risk of gang involvement are consistent across all ethnic and racial groups. These included low socioeconomic status, belonging to immigrant groups, discrimination, social isolation, limited education,

135. Justice & Meares, 2014
136. Justice & Meares, 2014; Seigel, 2011
137. Seigel, 2011
138. Ritter, Simon, Mahendra & U. S. OJP/NCIPC, 2013
139. Grebelsky-Lichtman, 2014; Yamauchi, 2010
140. Ritter et al., 2013

limited parental involvement, limited parental monitoring, and substance use.[141] A need for cultural identity is the primary driving force behind gang participation, but the significance of cultural identity is simultaneously torn away by these risk factors. These risk factors for gang involvement remain as consistent today as they were fifty years ago, but gang involvement is now becoming more racially and ethnically diverse.[142]

Many juveniles willingly become involved in gangs because they are looking for the sense of family involvement that they are not getting at home.[143] Many of these adolescents are on the streets because of abuse and neglect. Some are runaways of parents who are never around; many feel lost and insecure. They are looking for relationships in all the wrong places because they have not developed healthy relationships at home. Girls join gangs for much the same reasons that boys do, centering on aspects of deprivation and disengagement. Girls with low self-esteem find a sense of supportive relationships and commitment in gang involvement, but this is often a deception. A quarter of the girls surveyed had suspected mental health problems, and one-third were identified as at risk of suicide or self-harm. Girls involved in gangs were more likely to have experienced poor educational performance, neglect at home, violence at home, or sexual abuse.[144]

Parenting is the process of caring for a child while preparing the same for the basic roles, responsibilities, and challenges of life. Parents create the environment and experiences that facilitate healthy emotional, social, and cognitive development. Cultural influences create this as well, but culture is even more instrumental in guiding parents in what types of environments and experiences are created. Culture establishes deeprooted ideas of how each person should feel, think, and act in order to become a functional member of that society. Most cultures establish a

141. Ritter et al., 2013
142. Ritter et al., 2013
143. Allen, 2013; Ritter et al., 2013
144. Allen, 2013

set of scripts identifying behaviors and attitudes associated with proper parenting, usually including behaviors that are appreciated, emphasized, rewarded, discouraged, or punished. This suggests that studying parenting within a specific culture can provide insight into what constitutes good parenting and mental health for children.[145]

Parenting is so vital to child development and mental health because culture is so deeply influential on parenting. One of the most important things a parent does is determine the culture a child is born into. Culture has a great deal to do with the freedoms parents permit their children, the freedom to explore their surroundings and the corresponding repercussions if they go beyond what is expected. Culture determines how parents care for children, including how nurturing or restrictive they are. Cultural influences on parents and parenting are immensely important to child development and cognition from a very early age. The most important universal requirement for healthy parenting is that parents and children communicate with each other. This is vital to developing healthy and normal interactions along with maintaining good mental health.[146]

Parental interpretations of culture determine the conformity and behaviors of children in relation to cultural standards. Again, good mental health is generally identified by behaviors that conform to community and cultural expectations. As such, parents must have a healthy interpretation of cultural expectations. This helps them develop the parenting skills required to transfer the understanding of these expectations to the children, contributing to their children exhibiting good mental health.[147]

In the 1900s, psychologists and sociologists identified that parental abuse and neglect, parental influence, and the quality of parent-child interactions are all primary contributing factors to early childhood development, delinquency, mental health, and criminal behavior. This led to the development of the juvenile justice system and the judicial rationale of

---

145. Bornstein, 2013
146. Bornstein, 2013
147. Bornstein, 2013

parens patriae, the doctrine of dealing with delinquent children as a wise and merciful father would deal with his children.[148] In the latter part of the twentieth century, the primary response seemed to be principles associated with the phrase "It takes a village to raise a child." Raising children is not just the responsibility of parents; it is the responsibility of the community as a whole. The village principle seems to suggest that authorities must step in to take over the parenting role when parents are not consistent in their views of education, discipline, nutrition, exercise, and social awareness.[149] However, this principle has been distorted in many ways over the last twenty years. In my own experience, I have heard parents say, "It's not my responsibility to take care of my kids! It's everyone's—the village."

If we consider the "village" to be family, friends, neighbors, schools, industry, government, and all other aspects of the community we live in, then the village is vital to the lives of children. However, the purpose of the village is to hold parents accountable for the responsibility they have to raise healthy children into productive, happy adults, not to take over for parents, remove parental authority, or make all parenting consistent. In the process, parents who will not take responsibility for their role in their children's lives must be held accountable for their choices that bring harm to their children.[150] This harm may be physical, but more often it is emotional and psychological harm, the result of a rejected hug and a parent's expectations that exceed the physical, emotional, or cognitive capacity of the child.[151] Parenting will never be perfect, but it is the single greatest influence in any person's life. As such, the goal of society should not be to remove parental influence; it should be to promote and demand healthy parenting.

Parental influence can come in the form of biological parents, adoptive, blended, foster, and any other direct caregiver role. Optimal development

148. Bartol & Bartol, 2012b; Goldstein & Weiner, 2003; Taylor et al., 2007
149. Clinton, 1996
150. Kennair & Mellor, 2007; Taylor et al., 2007; Wallace & Roberson, 2011; Wolfe & McIsaac, 2011
151. Wallace & Roberson, 2011; Wolfe & McIsaac, 2011

from birth to five years is represented by breastfeeding, good parental mental health, family support, parental sensitivity, stimulation at home, and being read to at home. Developmental vulnerability is represented by biological susceptibility, premature birth, maternal smoking, poor child physical health, maternal depression, harsh parenting, poor stimulation, no preschool, and poverty.[152] One might conclude that more equality is needed in social capital, social services, and healthcare. However, the majority of inequity in development seems to have more to do with parental involvement and effort in their children's lives than a lack of social services and poverty. All of the positive and negative circumstances listed above occur in wealthy families as well as families in poverty.

Mental health professionals are realizing the "depth and complexity of emotional and behavioral disorders of America's children".[153] Traditionally, mental health professionals looked at families as the problem. There are often problems within families that do contribute to mental health disorders in children, but the traditional response was to pull children from their families and place them in intensive institutional treatment settings. As we become more aware of the true dynamics taking place within families, we now understand that the best approach is to keep families together and work to help the entire family rebuild rather than tear them apart. Even intensive treatment can take place in the home by wrapping services around a child and their family.[154]

Parenting behaviors require a combination of knowledge of all the things a child must understand about life. Good parenting behaviors also require the compassion to stop everything you are doing, no matter how important it is, to give a hug and wash off a skinned knee. It requires the self-control to understand that a child didn't have the ability to understand that throwing a ball in the living room could destroy that priceless family heirloom. Child-proofing a home is the process of changing things that

---

152. Woolfenden et al., 2013
153. Knitzer, 1993
154. Knitzer, 1993

might endanger a child along with removing things you don't want broken. Good parenting requires the servitude to get up from the couch to get a child a glass of milk, a snack, or a toy, even if that means you sit down and get back up a dozen times an hour. In many cases, poor parenting behaviors are often typical responses that some adults have toward any challenging circumstance.[155] With education and counseling, these normal but potentially harmful behaviors can be corrected in parents who may lack understanding but care enough about their children to desire to learn and improve.

Neglect is not always intentional. We often take simple life skills for granted. Parents who have trouble planning, poor anger management skills, poor self-control, depression, and no motivation often place children in negligent circumstances.[156] They leave children alone and unsupervised, or they fail to understand how to provide for the simple needs of children.[157] Children don't have tremendously complex needs. When they are hungry, they want something to eat. When they are cold, they want to be warm. When they fall, they want someone to pick them up. When they are scared, they want a hug and reassurance that everything is okay.

Children like to explore. They love to make noise and climb. Children will pull pots and pans out of the cupboards to use as drums. They won't realize the difference between a spatula with no sharp edges and the sharpest butcher knife in the drawer. The legal definition of neglect is an act or omission (something you failed to do but should have) leading to the harm or threat of harm to a child's health and well-being. Parents need to keep a close eye on their children, but you can't lock them up like prisoners.[158] Part of healthy development involves exploring their surroundings and learning by trial and error. The frustration for most parents is not the complexity of a child's needs but rather the fact that most children have

155. Wolfe & McIsaac, 2011
156. Wallace & Roberson, 2011; Wolfe & McIsaac, 2011
157. Jenny, 2011; Wallace & Roberson, 2011, Wolfe & McIsaac, 2011
158. Wallace & Roberson, 2011

constant needs. Most adults listen to the radio while driving rather than just drive in silence. The reason Facebook, Twitter, YouTube, Netflix, and other social media or entertainment web sites are so popular is because we are driven by a desire to be constantly entertained. Humans inherently desire instant gratification. In this way, adults are no different than children.

The difference is that the form of gratification and entertainment we desire changes as we mature from a child to an adult. As we mature, we become less dependent on others to supply our needs and an inherent desire for independence takes over. Adults still desire companionship and affection, but our inherent desire for independence drives adults to explore and reach out beyond the family for these desires. Children have not yet developed this independence; they are completely dependent on parents to provide for all of their needs and desires. This dependence can conflict with the adult desire for independence. Parents with substance abuse disorders, poor educational backgrounds, behavioral disorders, a history of abuse as a child, poor anger management, and other mental or physical health problems may easily develop neglectful or abusive responses to the dependence of their children. Single parents and parents of children with behavioral disorders, learning disabilities, physical disabilities, or other special needs are even more susceptible to developing neglectful or abusive reactions to the constant demand for attention.[159]

As a father, I am very proud of my children. I hope they are proud of me. My children are the greatest gifts I have ever received. Yet, they have also been the greatest challenge and test of patience. I have made plenty of mistakes with my children, and in the process, I needed to be willing to ask my kids to forgive me for getting upset when I shouldn't have. Children require discipline and guidance, but it must be done with love and compassion. Parents must be able to look at their children as they would customers—with an attitude of service. This can be extremely

---

159. Jenny, 2011, Wolfe & McIsaac, 2011

difficult to grasp, but children will always need more hugs than discipline.

We fail to recognize the frailty of young minds and the pain of young hearts that can occur from the simplest of things. We must make every effort to stop looking at children as fetuses and see them for how precious and valuable they really are. They are our hope for the future! Parents are the best hope for any child, and our efforts should be focused on using everything we have learned to help parents realize how important they are to their children.

FATHERS

CHOOSING TO HAVE CHILDREN IS the most important choice any two people will make. This decision requires two people; it is not something you do on your own. My kids are the greatest gift I have in life. They have brought more happiness to my life than anything else. I tell every young man I meet to wait to have kids until after he has been married for a couple of years and has created some financial stability. A young couple needs ample time spent together to really build their relationship before kids arrive, and being financially stable is naturally better for the well-being of the kids and the parents. Your kids will bring you more happiness than anything else in life if you really love them with all your heart. However, they will also bring more stress and require more energy than just about anything else in your life—no matter how much you love them.

My wife and I went to the doctor for a routine check the day our first son was born. He told us everything was fine and we had a few days to wait yet, but that night, my wife's water broke. After we got to the hospital, the staff noticed something was wrong. The baby was breech, and before I knew what was happening they were shipping my wife off to emergency surgery. This was definitely one of the scariest times of my life. Everything went well with the surgery, but the staff had trouble with the IV pumps and a variety of other problems occurred over the next couple of days. When we finally got in the car to leave the hospital with Brandon for the first time, the full power and weight of life hit me as I looked back at my wife and son. I realized then that everything I do, every choice I make in life will have an impact on this little boy.

He is completely dependent on us for everything: food, water, shelter, clothing, heat, cool, air quality, protection, safety, learning, understanding, love, kindness, respect, patience, fun, and exercise. Everything is completely dependent on us—on me. I don't just mean whether or not he falls down the stairs or wanders out into a busy street; we are responsible for his mental, emotional, and spiritual well-being. He needs all the love, affection, and time I can give. It is my responsibility to teach him right from wrong, but I can't expect too much from him too soon or be too harsh. My life suddenly revolved totally around my son. I was happier than I had ever felt before, yet at the same time, I felt considerable fear. I realized I had no idea how to be a dad.

We were all born with a purity of heart. Children have the ability to love unconditionally. A child trusts and believes everything you say. The innocent, pure heart of a child is inherently happy. The only things a child needs are food, protection, and the ability to give love. Kids don't care where they live as long as there is something to eat. The essentials in life are food, warmth, and protection from the storm. Kids don't generally care whether their clothes match, or even whether they are wearing clothes or not! As long as they are warm and comfortable, they are happy.

Love is essential to happiness in life. For a child who falls and scrapes a knee, the only thing that matters is having someone close by who can pick them up, give a hug and a smile, and say, "It's ok, it's only a little cut. I know it hurts, but you'll be ok." A child experiencing pain knows something is wrong but doesn't understand what exactly is going on. Generally, a child experiences more fear than physical pain in this situation. A child needs a hug more than a bandage most of the time. The pure heart of a child trusts and loves others. Unless a child is told otherwise, this pure, unconditional love will be automatically extended beyond just parents, family, and friends to all people.

Fear is a result of pain, both physical pain and emotional pain even more. A loving embrace (a hug, a gentle pat on the back, or holding hands) and a few words spoken with confidence ("It's ok. I know it hurts, but you'll be ok. I'll help you.") give the child the ability to know they don't have to be afraid. Children depend on parents and other adults for this love and protection. It builds confidence, strength, character, and the ability to cope with life's challenges. This is essential for little boys and girls to develop into healthy men and women who can then provide this love and protection to others as well.

If the child is told, "Stop whining! Stop crying! What did you do that for? That wasn't very smart. What's wrong with you?" this only creates confusion and more fear. If the child is looking for a hug for reassurance but is refused, there is nothing to take away the fear. When adults are angry or insensitive instead of loving and compassionate, nothing takes the fear away. This turns into anger. Anger destroys the child's purity of the heart, and their ability to trust is gradually destroyed.

This child will carry this wound into adulthood. It destroys their ability to trust others or have faith in someone. This destroys a person's ability to have healthy, loving relationships. We do the same thing with God. Faced with a challenge in life, we pray. When the end result isn't what we prayed it would be, we feel hurt. Angry at God, we lose faith.

The decision to have sex and make babies is taken lightly by so many these days. People don't think about or truly care about the choice they make; they just want to enjoy the fun of making babies but don't care about the child they create. This, in my opinion, may be the worst form of cruelty. Why? No matter how much a parent tries to hide it, no matter how much the parents try to make themselves feel it, a child always knows whether their father and mother genuinely care about them or not.

Until a child is old enough to understand the significance of God, someone they can't see, children are totally focused on the people closest to them, the people they are completely dependent on for everything. This creates an emotional bond. Children often can read their parents' minds and hearts with such clarity that they know the parents better than the parents know themselves. A child will always know how a parent really feels about them, and this will influence how the child feels about themselves and others.

This unconditional love provides a parent with a lot of grace. I have heard countless stories of children who were abused or neglected by their parents but never told anyone, or even lied to authorities, because they didn't want the parents to get hurt. We learn how to love from our parents, so they assume the abuse they experience is love. The parent directly or indirectly blames the child for their problems; the child in turn knows this and believes it. When this same child reaches adulthood, this will create a negative sense of self-worth and impact every relationship this man or woman will ever have.

A child's continued unconditional love for a parent allows for a tremendous amount of forgiveness. We are often able to find it in our hearts to forgive someone for something they did wrong, but we are not always able to forget the pain it created. If someone steals a dollar from you and then comes to you later to apologize, you can easily forgive them even if you don't get your dollar back. We can easily forget a small wrongdoing to the point that a couple months later, you might not even have a clue what the same person is talking about if they come to you to give back the dollar.

On the other hand, no one ever forgets the pain of a broken bone. Even after the wound is healed and life is completely back to normal, we never truly forget the pain of the event or the details of how it occurred. This may be more than the memory of the pain. It may be the frustration of dealing with life with only one hand or trying to get around on crutches. Beyond just the pain felt, the impact an event or act has on our normal life is often what we remember the most. This impact may be the fear that is created because of something that happened, especially when love and trust is turned into fear and uncertainty. In the Bible, Paul talks about creating healthy relationships between parents and children. He says children should respect and obey their parents in all things at all times. He also tells parents, "Do not provoke your children to become angry, because they will become discouraged" (Colossians 3:21).

Genealogies are an important, but very dull part of the Bible. It reflects what is important to God, the importance of fathers. Jesus is considered of the house of David. Joseph not Mary is from the genealogy of David even though Joseph never physically contributed to Jesus' birth. What does a father provide? He provides leadership, love and stability. He is an example of what a man should do and how a man should act. A father provides training in various skills related to work, hobbies or sports. For centuries all over the world, sons went to work each day with their fathers to help and learn. Today, fathers go to work every day and hardly ever see their children. A father provides stability by being fair. He provides safety and protection until the child grows up and can provide for self. You don't have to be the biological dad in order to be a great father to your kids. On the other hand, if all you provide is money, a house to live in, food on the table, clothes on their backs, and a birthday present each year, you really aren't being a father.

Kids need to know their dad is proud of them. Even if your kid screws up and does something wrong, sons and daughters need to know that Dad is still proud of what they have done right. Your kids need to hear it's OK to mess up at times—everyone does! It's always OK to make mistakes as long as you learn from your experiences and try to do better next time. Tell your kids you are proud they have the courage to try. A father must discipline his kids. You must find a way to help your kids understand what they did wrong, why it's wrong, and how to correct it. But your kids also need to know you are proud of them, that you love them, no matter what they do. A father must work to find every ounce of good he can possibly find in his kids and make sure they see it too.

The only way for you to be a truly loving parent is to learn to see and love your children with the same unconditional love that your children have for you—the same love God has for you.

You must ultimately come to the understanding that no one has any authority or control over your life; instead, it is determined by the decisions you make at any given moment in time. You may never know how many people are counting on you to make the most of every moment you have, but you should know that your children are at the top of the list.

THE SICKNESS IN AMERICA

THROUGHOUT THE CENTURIES, PUNISHMENTS FOR crime were often incredibly cruel and torturous. The intention was, indeed, for the punishment to be painful and public. In medieval Europe, people were drawn and quartered for murder and thieves had their hands cut off. Even into America's infancy, women were burned alive if they were accused of witchcraft. In the Wild West, hangings were the popular punishment for horse thieves. We look back now and view these acts as inhumane. Within the scope of our modern justice system, many are trying to eliminate capital punishment all together.

Much of the discussion around capital punishment has to do with pain and suffering or the rights of the criminal. Our entertainment industry floods our society with a constant stream of graphically violent movies and television shows. These include cable TV series like *The Walking Dead* and *Breaking Bad* and movies like the *Saw* series. Compared to the computerized graphics of modern horror films, the special effects of the original *Texas Chainsaw Massacre* seem cheesy, almost comical. The very interesting dynamic taking place in American social culture is that the same groups of people who create these incredibly violent and realistic shows for entertainment are often the same people who suggest that the death penalty is wrong.

The criminals we would be executing would presumably be the people who have actually committed horribly gruesome killings—in real life—similar to what these people are creating for entertainment. Even so, the discussion of the death penalty seems to always come down to morality and fairness.[160] This is the suggestion that people who have destroyed another person's right by inflicting horrible pain, suffering, and death still have the exact same rights as their victims. Emotions always run high on all sides when discussing death, so the emotional aspects usually take over the discussion. However, the real issue for debate is not the morality or fairness of the death penalty but why capital punishment exists at all.

All men are created equal and share the same rights. However, the only way for our criminal justice system to protect everyone equally is to take action against individuals who violate the rights of others. If an individual has chosen to harm or kill other people and shows no regard for other people's right to life, that person will likely kill again if given the opportunity.[161] The only way to insure such a person is refused the opportunity to commit further heinous acts is to lock them away in confinement until end of their life or the enactment of the death penalty. It seems the end result is the same, and the decades of confinement alone could actually be a far more cruel existence for the human spirit than death itself.

Death is not a punishment, as in death there is no opportunity for the person to correct their behavior. Looking back through history, we can see that this was obviously not the way most people felt. For the most part, capital punishment has always been a public spectacle. Historically, these public displays of hanging, burning, disemboweling, and so on have always taken place as community events. The whole countryside would come to town to have a family picnic of sorts and watch the ordeal, just as we watch violent TV shows, movies, and video games today. We attempt to discount this or justify ourselves by suggesting that movies and TV are not actually real and public executions of old were. The sad truth is that there really is no difference.

160. Newbauer, 2006
161. Seigel, 2011, pp. 103-104

We would never imagine taking children to an execution in modern times. In the days of old, these were important opportunities to teach children what happens when you harm other people or break the law. We all want to feel free and safe; we all want to see justice done. Even if the crime had nothing to do with me, I can believe that justice will be done in my life if I see justice done in someone else's life. There is a certain satisfaction, even pleasure, found in seeing a wrong made right. We all feel excited and cheer when we see the good guy defeat the bad guy in movies. Similarly, we also want to know that our leaders are working to protect us.

Many would like to think that we are better now that we fight against capital punishment, but we aren't. Our children watch the same graphic, bloody, up-close-and-personal sort of violence all the time, but there is no lesson to be learned anymore. It is just entertainment. Children don't understand what is right or wrong unless they are taught what is right and wrong, but children now watch death and violence for entertainment and parents don't take the time teach right and wrong anymore.

American Indian tribes used marijuana in ceremonies or as medicine. Cocaine comes from coca leaves. They were chewed by South American tribes for centuries as a medicine. Heroine was used as a medicine in Asia for centuries, and it was also used as a painkiller to minimize the suffering of the elderly and diseased. Many illicit drugs were used for medicine and ceremony through the centuries, but there were tribal medicine men or other community leaders who strictly regulated the use of these same substances. Drunkards and addicts who could not work or productively function in these societies were shunned by their peers. Those who committed crimes to support their addictions were punished.

The widespread acceptance of "recreational" drug use on a daily basis and the acceptance of dependency is something recent and unique to the twentieth century, the industrial age. Most adults drink, but they do not let it control their lives. The average American understands "I can't go out and get drunk tonight; I have to work in the morning." Adult recreational drinking does not always lead to alcoholism, and I would even go as far as to say that adult recreational drug use does not always lead to addiction. So, what influences determine going in one direction versus the other?

When we look at all of the influences that tend to create delinquency (e.g., abuse, neglect, chemical dependency, drugs for recreation, sex for recreation, sexual perversion for entertainment, and violent and bloody entertainment), we can see how these influences have also taken root in society as acceptable, even desirable, rights and freedoms.[162] Normally, a life of crime does not start once the person has become an adult. Most of the hardcore criminals in jail today started their life of crime as juveniles.

We encourage juveniles to explore their sexual curiosities before they are even old enough to responsibly care for, or care about, the babies that may result from such endeavors. Then we encourage young girls to destroy the babies with an abortion if something goes wrong. We see ads on TV all the time for various organizations trying to generate funds to save abused animals, but you never see an ad for an organization trying to help abused children. At the same time, we suggest that murderers have the same rights as the victim's family and more rights than the victim. What are we telling our youth? Babies aren't human and don't matter, animals are more important than people, and a murder victim is dead anyway, so they don't really matter anymore.

We fill our prisons with juveniles and minorities. These are people trying to sell a little marijuana on the street. Some of them do it so they can buy an expensive car and party with their friends; others just don't know any other way to get some money to buy food. The buyer who goes home to get high is ignored by the criminal justice system while his kids are living in filth and have nothing to eat. If one of the children gets in trouble for wandering the streets, the child is brought home to dad for a beating after the police leave. If the child eventually ends up in the hospital, the father is given self-esteem counseling and sent through chemical dependency

---

162. Taylor, 2007, pp.74-85

treatment at our expense. I personally believe the father who is getting high while neglecting and beating his kids should be in jail rather than the guy he bought the drugs from.

If you feel pain in your body, you go to the doctor for help. If the doctor tells you that you have cancer, you may be angry and fearful, but you plan for treatment. The desire is to get rid of the cancer as soon as possible, even though the treatment will be painful. Over the last several decades, America's core values have been under attack similar to the way cancer attacks the body. Unfortunately, we went to the wrong doctors. America continues to take the advice of leaders who tell us, "Don't worry, it's really not that bad." We allowed our leaders to convince us that we have the *right* to be sick because we did not want to go through the pain of treatment. Without any remediation, we passed the cancer on to our kids and it spread. Now, it is almost inoperable.

There isn't much some people can do to change their socioeconomic circumstances. Low income and poverty create very real hardships, but the vast majority of Americans work hard all their lives to scrape together a living. Children growing up in the inner city can be successful if they are encouraged to learn and work hard, but this requires consistent love and support from parents and teachers. Unfortunately, most of these children are told they are victims of circumstances beyond their control. They are told they will never amount to anything and there is nothing they can do about it, so don't even bother trying. Who tells them this? They learn it from their parents, teachers, and community leaders.

Again, make a list of all of the circumstances that we know contribute to juvenile delinquency. These include chemical dependency, recreational drug use, sexual promiscuity, teen pregnancy, and gang recruiting along with bloody, violent, and sexually perverted entertainment, to name just a few.[163] One hundred years ago, every item on this list was considered morally unacceptable or not normal. Now, almost every item is considered

---

163. Taylor, 2007

normal, socially acceptable, or morally neutral.

Beyond abuse and neglect, studies have shown that low parental involvement contributes to delinquency. Chemical dependency in the family, or even regular drug and alcohol use by parents, can also contribute to use and abuse in juveniles. Stress in the home, no parental presence, lack of discipline, and lack of a religious foundation in the home are high risk factors as well.[164] The vast majority of parents nurture and love their children; they want their children to be happy and healthy. The abuse and neglect of children is not a new phenomenon. Throughout history, children were looked at as property. Anything a child did was looked at as the responsibility of the parents. Anything the child did, good or bad, was considered to be a reflection on the parents. I bring this up purely as a point of reference. Discipline is important in any child's life, but the reality is that many parents discipline too harshly or not enough. Like most adults, you would consider it unfair for your employer to demand you do a job without any training and then fire you on the spot for doing the job incorrectly. We often forget that our children deserve the same consideration.

Many of these high-risk circumstances have more to do with the relationship between the parents than the relationship the parents have with the children. Psychologists and sociologists have conducted numerous research studies related to marriage and divorce. These studies have proven that marriage, the commitment between the father and mother, is vital to raising healthy children into adults. Children of two-parent households are healthier and less likely to be delinquent, and single moms are more likely to be in poverty and victims of crime than married women.[165]

This requires more than just a casual commitment. Research shows that cohabitation is not the functional equivalent of marriage. Children with parents who were living together but not married generally reflected statistical outcomes that were closer to the children of single parents rather

164. Taylor, 2007
165. Newbauer, 2006, p.132

than married parents. People who live together seem to have lower-quality relationships than married couples. Parents who cohabitate reported more conflict, more violence, less commitment, and lower levels of satisfaction compared to married couples. Even biological parents living together reported higher conflict and lower-quality relationships than married biological parents. After thirty years of sexual revolution, only 60 percent of American children live with their own two married biological parents.[166]

Throughout history, every known human society has had some form of marriage. This was more than just a romantic declaration or religious rite;[167] marriage served as a public act, a binding commitment. The traditional view was that sex outside of marriage was wrong. Who enforced this rule? It wasn't the government. Families enforced this rule. Throughout every complex society governed by law, the purpose of a legal marriage contract is to insure a man and woman make a commitment to provide for the children they produce.[168] One of the most significant problems we face is that marriage means nothing in America anymore. Divorce rates are on the rise in straight couples. Legal gay marriage is something fairly new. Even so, statistics reflect that gay couples are getting divorced at even higher rates. America needs to make a commitment to change our views on marriage and family.

One of the amendments on the Minnesota voting ballot for the 2012 election was the Marriage Amendment, establishing that marriage is a union of one man and one woman and stating that gay marriage is illegal. It also states that a man married to more than one woman (bigamy) is illegal and that an adult cannot marry a minor (pedophilia). Millions of people all over the nation are having sexual relations with whomever they want, whenever they want. People have the right to make their own choices, however risky and destructive those choices may be; written laws don't regulate or stop this. Again, the purpose of a common-law marriage

166. Gallagher, 2002, p. 777-779
167. Gallagher, 2002, p. 774
168. Gallagher, 2002

contract is to provide a legally recognized commitment between a man and woman to provide for the children they produce.

My parents divorced when I was fifteen. Fortunately, there were a lot of men who stepped up to the plate to help me through difficult times in my life as father figures and mentors. My mom then remarried an absolutely wonderful man a few years later. He has been Dad to me ever since. I know a lot of men who have married single mothers and adopted their children, and these men are great fathers and love these children as their own. Yet again, we can't ignore facts. Studies performed by psychologists and sociologists prove certain truths. Child abuse rates are much higher in blended families.[169] Statistically, biological fathers raising their children are less likely to abuse their children than a step-father or live-in boyfriend. In the majority of circumstances, the connection that a biological parent has with a child is different than the connection anyone else will ever have with that child. All of us do our entire society a disservice when we choose to discount the importance of both biological parents in a child's life.

The cancer in America started when we began telling parents, both mothers and fathers, that having a career was as important as or more important than being a parent. Divorce is acceptable. Sex has nothing to do with intimacy, love, and commitment; it is purely a means of personal gratification, and abortion is the answer to any problems. Chemical dependency and obesity really aren't your fault, because none of us are really strong enough to say no to anything anyway.

We are systematically destroying the moral standards that form the foundation of our freedoms. This destruction is the result of decades of attacks against our respect for life and the foundation of society. Long before there was any government, church, king, or court, there was the family. The village of friends and neighbors helping each other is helpful but not always necessary. The most important people in a child's life are Dad and Mom.

---

169. Siegel, 2011, p.274

Healthy families are the foundation of a healthy society. Governments, businesses, schools, citizens, and even churches must answer to parents. I have heard this discussed a number of times over the last few years, but there is another side of this issue that I have not heard anyone mention before. Citizens, churches, schools, businesses, and even governments must demand that parents care for the children they bring into this world.

This is more than just providing food and shelter. Our social standards must reflect the expectations we have of parents. My grudge against our social views on marriage and abortion is deeper than any political debate, as I have spent a lot of time over the years with people who were drug users, gangbangers, or suicidal because their moms told them "I wish I would have aborted you" or "I wish your father would have taken you with him when he left."

SO, WHAT CAN WE DO?

THE QUESTION WE MUST ASK is this: Why do we accept this? Why do we willingly allow destructive behavior to become acceptable or normal? The criminal justice system labels much of this behavior as victimless crime, indicating a belief that the only people who are harmed by the activity are the participants. Prohibition started in the 1920s because the nation's leadership felt alcohol was destroying the country. This *temperance movement* was widespread across all levels of society.[170]

Prohibition failed because it targeted the supply instead of the demand. Yet, it does reflect the social attitude that was prominent a century ago. The industrial age was changing how our society operated, how families operated. There were a lot of reasons for this, but it was convenient to blame increasing alcohol consumption rather than address the real problems.

We enjoy a level of freedom in America unlike the rest of the world could even comprehend. Our freedoms do not come from the government, as we have established a form of government that recognizes that people were born with God-given rights and freedoms long before any government was ever formed. The unfortunate reality is that freedom allows people to choose to harm others. Freedom allows us the right to do wrong. How do we counteract this?

Anytime you turn on the news, we hear people talking about their

---

170. 170 - Siegel, 2011

rights. Occupy Wall Street started out as a movement to fight against corruption on Wall Street. This was a grassroots movement drawing attention to people who use deceit to steal the retirement savings and wealth of other people. But despite this noble ideal, the movement deteriorated into a mob, demanding free everything while preventing citizens from getting to their jobs.

This was the result of a modern American phenomenon. The Occupy Wall Street protestors believed they had the right to protest but failed to realize the responsibility they had to respect the rights of other people. Their protest trampled on the rights of thousands of their fellow Americans who just wanted to go to work, make a living, go home to their families, and enjoy life. Americans seem to have adopted the idea that our rights as individuals are more important than our responsibility to respect the rights of others. We fail to realize, or adequately teach future generations, that we have no rights unless we all assume the responsibility to respect other people's rights as equally important, or even more important, than our own.

The War on Drugs was also a failure, just as Prohibition was. Both were attempts to influence people's behavior by eliminating the supply of a product, but there will always be a supply as long as there is demand. So, how do we influence demand? We require people to take responsibility for their actions.

If people want to get drunk and high on the weekend, that is the choice of each individual. However, you better be clean by the time you go back to work. If your coworkers or children suffer because of your recreational activities, you should be held responsible. If someone is harmed because you believed your right to recreational activity was more important than your responsibility to the safety of others, your actions are criminal. Drug testing for any workplace accident, whether injuries are present or not, should be law. Employers should have the right to terminate employment if the employee tests positive as being under the influence. The employee should lose their workers' compensation insurance as well.

The first step is for us to establish what the right to life really is through a constitutional amendment. Any organism that forms into a person and cannot form on its own without some contribution from both a man and woman constitutes life. As such, this life has the right to live, grow, and prosper. All too often, pro-choice and pro-life supporters fail to accept the very cold, hard facts that must be understood when discussing the issue of abortion.

I have spent a lot of time with women who have miscarried unexpectedly or chose to have an abortion for any number of reasons. The medical and psychological complications that result from abortion are real; every abortion is a very traumatic experience for the mother. No one will ever be able to convince me otherwise. Politicians and special interest groups on both sides have made this very traumatic issue one of the loudest political discussions in history, but they fail to consider that they are just rubbing salt in millions of already open wounds.

The life of a mother carrying this life inside her must be the priority. Any woman facing serious medical complications during pregnancy will think about this after being told by a doctor, "You survived this time. If you choose to continue this pregnancy, you may very well die before you ever make it to the hospital if this happens again." A fetus is a baby. A baby has a right to life, but the mother's survival must be the priority. You can try to say that medical technology and social service programs virtually guarantee that a child can survive and be cared for even if the mother does not survive, and yes, that is true—if she makes it to the hospital. Millions of women have made the traumatic decision to abort a pregnancy after experiencing severe healthcare complications, and these same women are forced to relive the trauma every time they see a group of people marching down the street in vagina costumes. Both sides have lost a sense of compassion for the women they presume to represent.

The life inside the mother is not the exclusive responsibility of the mother. This life is the responsibility of the father as well. This requires that both mother and father have a right to decisions made regarding this life along with joint responsibility to the safety, care, love, discipline and education of that life. Any decision to remove life support from a minor must be the joint decision of the mother, father and doctor. The law in most states says that a doctor cannot prescribe medication, examine or perform surgery on a minor without the parent's consent, the only exceptions being a life threatening emergency or suspected abuse. Yet, teenage girls in most states can now get birth control pills and abortions without parents knowing anything about it.

If the speed limit is fifty, there will still be people who drive faster. On most interstates, the limit is seventy, but there is also a minimum of forty. Freedom allows us to choose to do the wrong thing. Speed limit laws establish the safe standard for people to follow; the law does not and cannot prevent someone from speeding. The government can do nothing to prevent someone from speeding, and we can't prevent it either. Laws set a standard of what is acceptable and what is not, but they do nothing until after someone breaks the law.

Rape laws do not prevent a woman from being raped. There are two things that prevent a woman from being raped: a potential rapist's fear of the consequences and the respect the rest of us have for her rights. Our respect for her rights is something we establish in laws that determine what will happen to anyone who violates those rights, but the law does not stop rape. Lawmakers create laws based on constitutional rights. However, laws are also created based on their understanding of what is socially acceptable. Who determines what is socially acceptable? We do.

We have lost our concept of moral standards. In many cases, it is difficult for a woman to press charges for rape anymore. As a society, we accept that pretty much anything goes when it comes to sex and dating. We have no standard of what we consider acceptable behavior from men or women when it comes to relationships, be it dating, sex, marriage, fidelity, commitment, and so on. As a result, our automatic response to most rape victims is scrutiny. Did she really say no? When did she say no? This is a horrible state of affairs in America.

Abortion laws will not prevent or allow abortions. Gun laws will not prevent death any more than murder laws do. Our standards of what we will accept from each other prevent harm in our lives. We don't enforce these standards with guns, protests, or happy thoughts; we enforce these standards by helping each other through tough times while also demanding that every person take responsibility for their own actions.

WHAT WILL YOU DO?

THERE IS A SCENE IN the movie *Evan Almighty*. God (Morgan Freeman) is talking with Evan's wife (Lauren Graham) in a dinner and says something like this: If someone prays for patience, do you think God just gives the person patience, or do you think he gives the person an opportunity to be patient? If people pray for courage, do you think God just gives them courage, or does he give them an opportunity to be courageous? If you ask God to bring your family closer together, do you think God gives them warm fuzzy feelings, or does he give the family opportunities to show each other love, the opportunity to enjoy time together so their relationships grow stronger? Think about that for a minute. Let it sink in. Life's most intense problems often have simple solutions, but the solutions still may not be easy.

When a young soldier walks onto the battlefield for the first time, he knows he will face danger. Every firefighter is told stories of other firefighters who lost their lives because they ran into a burning building to save someone but never made it out. I am grateful that I have had the chance to meet quite a few heroes. Some were soldiers, like my grandfather, who stood up and charged the enemy so everyone else could get to cover. Another was a woman who ran up to a burning car to grab an injured driver.

In each case, the hero was an ordinary person who made a choice. "If someone doesn't do something, that guy is going to die. I may not be able to save him. I may die in the process, but I am going to do it anyway, I have to try!"

Many will say this takes a unique kind of courage. What it really takes is a very unique kind of love, the love that creates the courage a man needs to say, "I'm not going to the bar tonight. I am going home to read a book to my children." This is the kind of courage we desperately need in this country right now.

We all search for happiness and love, but many of us never truly find it because we look for it in the wrong things or for the wrong reason. This leads to an empty feeling because it is based on making *me* happy rather than a desire to make others happy.

God designed people to love and serve each other. True happiness comes from experiencing the gratitude and satisfaction we receive back from the people we give to. Give some groceries to a family because the dad just lost his job. Take a week off of work to help hurricane or earthquake victims, and take your family with you if you can. You may have the opportunity to risk your own life someday by running into a burning building to pull out a small child or an elderly man. Even something as simple as buying a guy a cup of coffee, taking the time to listen to his frustrations with life, can make a world of difference in his life. Taking the time to encourage him and listen, to be a friend.

True love is not something we get from other people; it is something we give to others, whether we receive it back or not.

As I have talked with men of all ages over the years, I have found the older generations seem to have more of the answers to life, love, commitment, and sacrifice than most. It would seem that facing the hardships of the Great Depression and WWII created a sense of urgency or a need to ask life's tougher questions. In the process, this generation seemed to have a greater understanding of the need to place others before themselves. This type of love for our fellow man, our neighbors, has not been found

WHAT WILL YOU DO?

much in our country over the last few decades. Some call it patriotism, yet this patriotism goes beyond just love of country. It creates in us a need to stand up for others who can't stand up for themselves.

Although they probably don't realize it, we are starting to notice this love for others and patriotism in a new generation—the generation of folks who have gone to war and the families they leave behind. They have seen how grateful the people in other countries are when someone stands by their side to fight for freedom, when men and women come from the other side of the globe to help. Not just to fight, but to help teach them how to fight. Not just through combat, but through the democratic process: voting, healthy debate of ideas, and putting aside petty differences to work together for the benefit of every man. The strength that doesn't run away when things get tough, and the compassion that sticks around after the fight is over to help clean up the mess.

Of all the questions we ask in life about why things happen the way they do, there is really only one question that is important. I believe this is the only real question God asks of us: "What will you do?" When it seems like you are facing hell, staring the devil right in the face, will you be ready? When someone else is going through tough times, will you be ready to serve? To sacrifice your time and energy to help? When someone else is facing danger, will you be ready to fight? Even more, will you be ready to listen? When the devil is shouting in your ear to do the wrong thing, will you be ready to hear the still, quiet, gentle voice telling you to have faith and do what you know is right? Not just the physical battles, but the intellectual battles we all must be willing to fight?

If not, you need to pray. Pray while you take a shower. Pray while you drive to work. Pray while you walk up the stairs or ride in the elevator. And, yes, pray in school! You don't have to pray out loud; He still knows what you are thinking. Open a Bible and actually read it. If you are not sure what you are reading, try going to church. Ask someone to explain it to you. This doesn't mean you won't make any more mistakes. You inevitably will. You won't be perfect, but you will know you don't have to be.

The problems in our nation are not due to politics or politicians, corporations or executives, oil companies, banks, gangs, or terrorists. There is one fundamental root cause of all our nation's problems. We have forgotten the foundation of leadership on which everything is built: the family, Dad, Mom, and the kids.

Before any nation, government, law, or religion was ever established, there was the family. Before any king, pharaoh, president, congressman, dictator, judge, pastor, priest, or executive existed, there was Dad. A father is the foundation of leadership. All other leadership in the nation is dependent on fathers being leaders in the home, but you can't truly lead until you understand that you answer to a higher authority as well.

Dad loves his wife and kids more than he loves himself. His family's needs are more important to him than his own desires. You need to provide food, shelter, clothing, and education for your loved ones, and you need to teach your kids right from wrong and spend time having fun with them.

We cannot expect other people to provide for our families anymore. Men need to stop expecting others to be a husband and father for them. Men must take responsibility for their actions, ask their loved ones to forgive them, and start rebuilding their lives with their children now. If the government were to collapse and our societal structure as we know it was wiped out, we would be left with the foundation it was built upon in the first place: the family. But only the strong families would survive. When the family fails, the rest of the nation fails as well.

We will always have people who are poor or lose their jobs. Before government welfare plans, people went to the church and family for help. Orphanages, food bank , and other private organizations helped those who were down on their luck. People gave to these organizations because they knew it might be them looking for help someday, or perhaps they already had been at one point in life.

If you are so lucky as to have people in your life who love you in spite of your faults, don't throw that love back in their faces. Soak it up like a sponge and love them back a hundred times more, especially your kids. If you don't know how to love them, ask God to teach you. Be honest with the people you care about and ask them to teach you how to love them.

Even if you think you don't have anyone around to love you, you must remember that God loves you more than any person ever could. Even though you can't see or touch Him, if you really believe in Him, pray to Him, and seek Him, you will feel His arms around you. You must realize that someone out there needs you to care. Some teenager somewhere is just waiting for you to care enough to play ball with them and listen.

These principles of love, faith, and sacrifice come down to this: You are important. You won't find happiness in life if you spend your life trying to make yourself happy. Love, faith, and freedom require you to act. Stand up and fight—not against each other, but for each other. Do something about the problems you see around you. You could go to a restaurant and order the biggest steak they have with a lobster tail and a cold beer, and it would taste really good. Or you could go to the grocery store, buy a bag of groceries for your unemployed neighbor, and then order a small steak with a cold beer, and the small steak will taste even better. Of course, you won't know who needs the groceries unless you take the time to go out and meet your neighbors.

Don't let anyone tell you that you can't change the world. You change your life, and you will change someone else's at the same time. Don't miss out on the chance to risk everything in order to make a difference in someone else's life. You may just find it was the greatest thing you ever did.

REFERENCES

Bible references are not direct quotes from a specific version. They are references to the location of a common word or phrase found in most versions.

Allen, D. (2013). Why girls fall into gang culture. *Nursing Children & Young People*, 25, 8, 8-9.

American Psychiatric Association (2013) *Diagnostic and Statistical Manual of Mental Disorders, 5th ed.* Arlington, VA: American Psychiatric Association.

Anwar, Z., Sandrine, T. (2012-09-01). Nutrition, adult hippocampal neurogenesis and mental health. *British medical bulletin*, 103, 1, 89-114.

Babcock, J. C., Miller, S. A. & Siard, C. (June 2003). Toward a typology of abusive women: Differences between partner-only and generally violent women in the use of violence. *Psychology of Women Quarterly*, 27, 2, 153-161.

Bartol, C.R., Bartol, A.M. (2012). *Current perspectives in forensic psychology and criminal behavior.* Los Angeles: SAGE Publications.

Bartol, C.R., Bartol, A.M. (2012). *Introduction to forensic psychology, research and application.* Los Angeles: SAGE Publications.

Bhar, S. S. & Brown, G. K. (2011; 2012). Treatment of depression and suicide in older adults. *Cognitive and Behavioral Practice*, 19, 1, 116.

Bornstein, M. H. (2013). Parenting and child mental health: a cross-cultural perspective. *World Psychiatry*, 12, 3, 258-265.

Brady, K. T. & Sinha, R. (2005). Co-occurring mental and substance use disorders: The neurobiological effects of chronic stress. *The American Journal of Psychiatry*, 162, 8, 1483-93.

Clinton, H. R. (1996). *It takes a village: And other lessons children teach us* (1st Touchstone ed.). New York: Simon & Schuster.

Desrosiers, A., Sipsma, H., Callands, T., Hansen, N., Divney, A., Magriples, U. & Kershaw, T. (January 01, 2014). "Love hurts": romantic attachment and depressive symptoms in pregnant adolescent and young adult couples. *Journal of Clinical Psychology*, 70, 1, 95-106.

Doba, K., Nandrino, J.-L., Dodin, V. & Antoine, P. (January 01, 2014). Is there a family profile of addictive behaviors? Family functioning in anorexia nervosa and drug dependence disorder. *Journal of Clinical Psychology*, 70, 1, 107-117.

Dog, T. (2010). The role of nutrition in mental health. *Alternative Therapies in Health & Medicine*, 16, 2, 42-46.

Eytan, A. (2011). Religion and mental health during incarceration: a systematic literature review. *Psychiatric Quarterly*, 82, 4, 287-295.

Ferguson, H. (July 01, 2012). Fathers, child abuse and child protection. *Child Abuse Review*, 21, 4, 231-236.

For-Wey, L., Bih-Ching, S., Tung-Liang, C. & Shio-Jean, L. (2009). Parental mental health, education, age at childbirth and child development from six to 18 months. *Acta Paediatrica*, 98, 5, 834-841.

Friedmann, P. D., Taxman, F. S. & Henderson, C. E. (April-2007). Evidence-based treatment practices for drug-involved adults in the criminal justice system. *Journal of Substance Abuse Treatment*, 32, 3, 267-277

Gallagher, M. (spring 2002). What is Marriage For? The Public Purpose of Marriage Law. *Louisiana Law Review*, 62(3), 5-6. Retrieved October 26, 2018, from https://digitalcommons.law.lsu.edu/lalrev/vol62/iss3/3/.

Garfinkel, L. (November, 2010). Improving family involvement for juvenile offenders with emotional/behavioral disorders and related disabilities, *Behavioral Disorders*, 36, 1, 52-60.

Gibb, B. E., Alloy, L. B., Abramson, L. Y., Rose, D. T., Whitehouse, W. G. & Hogan, M. E. (2001). Childhood maltreatment and college students' current suicidal ideation: A test of the hopelessness theory. *Suicide & Life-Threatening Behavior*, 31, 4, 405-415.

Gleason, M. M., Fox, N. A., Drury, S., Smyke, A., Egger, H. L., Nelson, C. A. & Zeanah, C. H. (2011). Validity of evidence-derived criteria for reactive attachment disorder: Indiscriminately Social/Disinhibited and emotionally Withdrawn/Inhibited types. *Journal of the American Academy of Child & Adolescent Psychiatry*, 50, 3, 216-231.

Goldstein, A. M., Weiner, I. B. (2003). *Handbook of psychology*. Volume 11, Forensic Psychology. Canada; John Wiley & Sons, Inc.

Grebelsky-Lichtman, T. (January, 2014). Parental patterns of cooperation in parent-child interactions: The relationship between nonverbal and verbal Communication. *Human Communication Research*, 40, 1, 1-29.

Grisso, T. (2008). Adolescent offenders with mental disorders. *The Future of Children*, 18, 2, 143-164

Gutiérrez-Lobos, K., Eher, R., Grünhut, C., Bankier, B., Schmidl-Mohl, B., Frühwald, S. & Semler, B. (February 01, 2001). Violent sex offenders lack male social support. *International Journal of Offender Therapy and Comparative Criminology*, 45, 1, 70-82.

Harbottle, L. (2011). Nutrition and mental health: the importance of diet in depression. *British Journal of Well-being*, 2, 7, 19-22.

Henslin, J. M. (2008). *Sociology: A down-to-earth approach, Ninth Edition*. Boston: Pearson/Allyn and Bacon.

Holt, C. (2001). The correctional officer's role in mental health treatment of youthful offenders. *Issues in Mental Health Nursing*, 22, 2, 173-180.

Isenberg-Grzeda, E., Kutner, H. E. & Nicolson, S. E. (2012). Wernicke-Korsakoff-syndrome: under-recognized and under-treated. *Psychosomatics,* 53, 6, 507.

Jenny, C. (2011). *Child abuse and neglect; diagnosis, treatment and evidence.* St. Louis; Elsevier Saunders.

Johnson, S. D., Stiffman, A., Hadley-Ives, E. & Elze, D. (2001). An analysis of stressors and co-morbid mental health problems that contribute to youths' paths to substance-specific services. *The Journal of Behavioral Health Services & Research*, 28, 4, 412-26.

Justice, B. & Meares, T. L. (2014). How the criminal justice system educates citizens. *The Annals of the American Academy of Political and Social Science*, 651, 1, 159-177.

Kafka, M. P. & Hennen, J. (2003). Hypersexual desire in males: Are males with paraphilias different from males with paraphilia-related disorders? *Sexual Abuse: A Journal of Research and Treatment*, 15, 4, 307-321.

Kennair, N., & Mellor, D. (2007). Parent abuse: a review. *Child Psychiatry & Human Development*, 38, 3, 203-219.

Knitzer, J. (1993). Children's mental health policy: challenging the future. *Journal of Emotional & Behavioral Disorders*, 1, 1, 8-16.

Knox, J. (2012). The impact of early life trauma on health and disease - By Ruth Lanius, Eric Vermetten and Clare Pain. *British Journal of Psychotherapy*, 28, 1, 132-135.

Lloyd, C. E. (2010, August). Diabetes and mental health; the problem of co-morbidity. *Diabetic Medicine*. 27, 8, 853-854.

Louden, J. E., Skeem, J. L., Camp, J. & Christensen, E. (2008). Supervising probationers with mental disorder. How do agencies respond to violations? *Criminal Justice and Behavior*, 35, 7, 832-847.

McCloskey, L. A., Figueredo, A. J. & Koss, M. P. (1995). The effects of systemic family violence on children's mental health. *Child Development*, 66, 5, 1239-1261.

McNamara, D. (2007). Co-occurring mental illness: early intervention matters. *Clinical Psychiatry News*, 35, 7, 22-22.

Morgan, R. D., Fisher, W. H., Duan, N., Mandracchia, J. T. & Murray, D. (2010). Prevalence of criminal thinking among state prison inmates with serious mental illness. *Law and Human Behavior*, 34, 4, 324-36.

Morgan, T. B., Crane, D., Moore, A. M. & Eggett, D. L. (2013). The cost of treating substance use disorders: individual versus family therapy. *Journal of Family Therapy*, 35, 1, 2-23.

Newbauer, D.W. (2006) *Debating Crime: Rhetoric and Reality*. Thompson Wadsworth. Belmont California.

Powers, A., Ressler, K. J. & Bradley, R. G. (January 01, 2009). The protective role of friendship on the effects of childhood abuse and depression. *Depression and Anxiety*, 26, 1, 46-53.

Ritter, N., Simon, T. R., Mahendra, R. R., United States. Office of Justice Programs & National Center for Injury Prevention and Control (US). (2013). *Changing course: preventing gang membership*. Washington, DC: U.S. Department of Justice, Office of Justice Programs.

Roskes, E., Feldman, R., Arrington, S. & Leisher, M. (1999). A model program for the treatment of mentally ill offenders in the community. *Community Mental Health Journal*, 35, 5, 461-72; discussion 473-5.

Sabri, B. (2012). Severity of victimization and co-occurring mental health disorders among substance using adolescents. *Child & Youth Care Forum*, 41, 1, 37-55.

Sandler, I. N., Wheeler, L. A. & Braver, S. L. (January, 2013). Relations of parenting quality, interparental conflict, and overnights with mental health problems of children in divorcing families with high legal conflict. *Journal of Family Psychology*: Jfp: Journal of the Division of Family Psychology of the American Psychological Association (division 43), 27, 6, 915-24.

Schubert, C. A., Mulvey, E. P. & Glasheen, C. (2011). Influence of mental health and substance use problems and criminogenic risk on outcomes in serious juvenile offenders. *Journal of the American Academy of Child and Adolescent Psychiatry*, 50, 9, 925-937.

Seigel, L.J. (2011). *Criminology: the core, 4th Edition.* Belmont, California: Wadsworth Cengage Learning

Sousa, C., Herrenkohl, T., Moylan, C., Tajima, E., Klika, J., Herrenkohl, R. & Russo, M. (January 01, 2011). Longitudinal study on the effects of child abuse and children's exposure to domestic violence, parent-child attachments, and antisocial behavior in adolescence. *Journal of Interpersonal Violence*, 26, 1, 111-136.

Sterling, S., Chi, F. & Hinman, A. (2011). Integrating care for people with co-occurring alcohol and other drug, medical, and mental health conditions. *Alcohol Research & Health: The Journal of the National Institute on Alcohol Abuse and Alcoholism*, 33, 4, 338-349.

Strike, C., Rudzinski, K., Patterson, J. & Millson, M. (2012). Frequent food insecurity among injection drug users: correlates and concerns. *BMC Public Health*, 12, 1, 1058-1058.

Taylor, R. W., Fritsch, E. J. & Caeti, T. J. (2007). *Juvenile justice; policies, programs and practices, 2nd Edition.* Boston: McGraw Hill Higher Education.

Telles, S., Singh, N. & Balkrishna, A. (2012). Managing mental health disorders resulting from trauma through yoga: A review. *Depression Research and Treatment*, 2012, 401513-9.

Tomlinson, D., Wilkinson, H. & Wilkinson, P. (September, 2009). Diet and mental health in children. *Child and Adolescent Mental Health*, 14, 3, 148-155.

Twenge, J. M. (2011). Generational differences in mental health: Are children and adolescents suffering more, or less? *American Journal of Orthopsychiatry*, 81, 4, 469-472.

Underwood, L. A., Barretti, L., Storms, T. L. & Safonte-Strumolo, N. (2004). A review of clinical characteristics and residential treatments for adolescent delinquents with mental health disorders: a promising residential program. *Trauma, Violence & Abuse*, 5, 3, 199-242.

Vanaelst, B., De, V. T., Huybrechts, I., Rinaldi, S. & De, H. S. (May 01, 2012). Epidemiological approaches to measure childhood stress. *Pediatric and Perinatal Epidemiology*, 26, 3, 280-297.

Wallace, H. & Robertson, C. (2011). *Family violence; legal, medical and social perspectives, Sixth Edition.* Boston; Allyn & Bacon.

Wolfe, D. A. & McIsaac, C. (January 01, 2011). Distinguishing between poor/dysfunctional parenting and child emotional maltreatment. *Child Abuse & Neglect*, 35, 10, 802-13.

Wong-Goodrich, S. (2010). Mechanisms by which early nutrition influences spatial memory, adult neurogenesis, and response to hippocampal injury. (Order No. 3398164, Duke University). ProQuest Dissertations and Theses, 321.

Woolfenden, S., Goldfeld, S., Raman, S., Eapen, V., Kemp, L. & Williams, K. (September, 2013). Inequity in child health: the importance of early childhood development. *Journal of Paediatrics and Child Health*, 49, 9.

Yamauchi, C. (June, 2010). Parental investment in children: differential pathways of parental education and mental health. *Economic Record*, 86, 273, 210-226.

Yoo, J. A. & Huang, C.-C. (January, 2013). Long-term relationships among domestic violence, maternal mental health and parenting, and preschool children's behavior problems. *Families in Society*, 94, 4, 268-276.

Zubaran, C., Fernandes, J. G. & Rodnight, R. (1997). Wernicke-Korsakoff syndrome. *Postgraduate Medical Journal*, 73, 855, 27-31.

THANK YOU

I WOULD LIKE TO THANK a few of the great men who have made a difference in my life. Men who took time to teach me what a great man is by being an example of the same.

Arnold Riemer Sr. (2001)

Frank Howenstein (2013)

William Ritter

Jonathan Patterson (2008)

Gregory Sherrill (2017)